AN INTRODUCTION TO INTELLECTUAL PROPERTY

Other books by the author:

Civil Liberties in England and Wales	ISBN 0-595-66572-1
Legal and Regulatory Framework for Business in the UK	ISBN 0-595-66573-X
UK Steel industry and International Trade	ISBN 0-595-32164-X

AN INTRODUCTION TO INTELLECTUAL PROPERTY

ESSAYS AND MATERIALS

Sally Ramage Dabydeen

iUniverse, Inc.

New York Lincoln Shanghai

AN INTRODUCTION TO INTELLECTUAL PROPERTY
ESSAYS AND MATERIALS

iUniverse, Inc.

For information address:
iUniverse, Inc.
2021 Pine Lake Road, Suite 100
Lincoln, NE 68512
www.iuniverse.com

ISBN: 0-595-32927-6

Printed in the United States of America

I dedicate this book to my six children, Edward, Michael, Angela, Timothy, Charlotte and David.

I hope it will spur them on to an academic life as I hope it will do for all those who think that educational achievements are only for the rich. I myself have known dire poverty and severe disability and I have struggled through life and fought adversity through study and education; to be free is to be free in mind. I hope that I can show that education and qualifications can never be taken away from you.

CONTENTS

CASES

A v B (2002) EWCA Civ 337; [2002] 3 WLR 542

AG v Guardian Newspapers (No. 2) [1990] AC

Airey v Ireland 2 EHRR 305

American Cyanamid v Ethicon [1975] AC 396

Annabel's v Schock [1972] RPC 838(CA)

Aristoc Ltd v Rysta Ltd [1945] AC 68

Ashdown v Sunday Telegraph Group Ltd [2001] EWCA Civ 1142; [2002] QB 546

Associated Newspapers plc v Newsgroup Newspapers Ltd [1986] RPC 515

Australian Broadcasting Corp v Lench Game Meats [2001] HCA 63

B Berezovsky and N Glouchkov v Forbes Inc & JW Michaels [2001] EWCA Civ 1251

Basset v SACEM [1987] ECJ in Case 402/85, ECR 1747

Bassey v Icon Entertainment PLC [1995] EMLR 596

Beloff v Pressdram [1973] 1 All ER 241

BP Amoco v John Kelly Ltd [2001]NI 25

Broadcasting Complaints Commission ex parte Granada Television Ltd TLR 16/12/94

BUMA/Stema v KaZaA 28/3/2002 Amsterdam

Cadbury Schweppes v FBI Foods [2000] FSR 491 at p 504 (Supr. Ct. of Canada)

Cambridge Nutrition v BBC [1990] 3 All ER 523

Campbell v MGN Ltd [2002] EWCA 1373

Colorcoat Trade Mark [1990] B of Trade RPC 511

Coco v AN Clark [1969] RPC 41

Douglas and Hello v OK Magazine & others [2001] FSR 732

Re Dualit Trade Mark [1999] The Times 19th July

Electronic Technique v Critchley [1997] FSR 401

EUROLAMB Trade Mark [1997] RPC 279

Fylde Microsystems Ltd. v Key Radio Systems Ltd. [1998] FSR 449; The Times, February 18, 1998; [1998] EIPR N-100

Handyside v UK, Series A, No. 24; 1 EHRR 737 (1979–80)

Hoechst v Chemiculture [1993] FSR 270

STATUTES AND CONVENTIONS

Agreement on Trade-related Aspects of Intellectual Property Rights, Including Trade in Counterfeit Goods (*The TRIPS agreement*) 33 ILM 1994
American Convention of Human Rights
Audio Home Recording Act (US)
Berne Convention for the Protection of Literary and Artistic Works 1886 & 1971
Canadian & Quebec Charter 1956
Convention for the Protection of Producers of Phonograms Against Unauthorised Duplication of their Phonograms
Copyright Act 1709
Copyright Act 1956
Copyright, Design & Patents Act 1988
Copyright & Related Rights Regulations UK
Council Directive 92/100 on rental right and lending right and on certain rights relating to copyright in the field of intellectual property [1992] O.J. L346/61
Council Directive 93/83 on the co-ordination of certain rules concerning copyright and rights related to copyright applicable to satellite broadcasting and cable retransmission [1993] O.J. L290/9
Council Directive 93/98/EEC of 29 October 1993 harmonising the term of protection of copyright and certain related rights.
Council Directive 95/44 EC 1995
Data Protection Act 1998
"Diplomatic Impunity" case, Report No. 11/96, case 11.230-Chile, May 3 1996 (Appeal to the Inter American Commission on Human Rights)
European Convention on Human Rights 1950
General Agreement on Tariffs and Trade (GATT)
Human Rights Act 1998
International Convention for the Protection of Performing Artists, Producers of Phonograms and Broadcasting Organisations
Multilateral Trade Negotiations (The Uruguay Round)
Public Lending Right Act 1979

Revised Berne Convention
Trade Related Aspects of Intellectual Property Rights 1992
UK Copyright, etc and Trade Marks (Offences & Enforcement) Act 2002
Universal Declaration on Human Rights 1948
US Digital Millennium Copyright Act (H.R.2281, 105th Congress
WIPO Copyright Treaty 1996

PREFACE

Intellectual property law has branches of patent law, trade mark law, design law and copyright law. It is not easy to prevent others from using your ideas or information for gain unless you use the sophisticated and esoteric legal techniques of intellectual property law. Those persons who undertake scientific and technical research or who create or interpret works of learning need legal protection against competitors. Copyright is especially important.

Copyright is a form of protection afforded to many different types of work. Copyright protection for literary work is well known, and this regime also applies to musical and artistic works, broadcasts, sound and video recordings and typographical arrangements. The aim of copyright is to protect the author's reputation by way of moral rights and the owner's economic interests in the work.

This book is an introduction to topics in intellectual property law by the unusual method of using moots, mock trials, questions and answers and essays. It is not a text book. It serves to interest the inquisitive, without going into the deep law of IP. I hope that reading it will make you want to read an IP text book and, for students, will make you decide to choose the subject for study.

INTRODUCTION

This book is on Intellectual Property which is a subject few know about and which is considered to be a subject only the elite of the legal profession practice. I have aimed in this book to bring the subject alive by using examples of Moots to show the meaning of the law, questions that we all want answers to. I have included cases to show how important the subject is to businesses; it is all a question of money. The Western world has well and truly captured the commercial value of intellectual property and the third world mostly is ignorant of their rights and the value of what they possess by way of their culture, stories, medicines and herbs, the content in their land and recipes that they have had passed down through the centuries. Mostly in Intellectual Property matters, the rich are the winners and the little man loses.

In the UK, it is only in the past fifteen years that most of Intellectual Property law has been passed whilst Europe has had IP laws for over a hundred years. Before the past fifteen years, the only IP law in the UK was the 1949 Registered Designs Act and the 1977 Patents Act.

It can be argued that there is too much IP law in the Western world, but I hope that this book will give the reader a taste of issues that are called Intellectual Property and raise awareness of IP law that is steadfastly creeping into all corners of our lives.

INTRODUCTION TO UK INTELLECTUAL PROPERTY

2004 IP MOOT—A Professor who Stole a Student's Work (the facts and the appellant's case)

**Oxford Intellectual Property Research Centre
and Intellectual Property Institute
International Intellectual Property Moot 2004**

FACT SITUATION

Professor J.R. Tookagain teaches a popular creative writing course at the University of Erewhon. He is also a well-known writer of popular fiction. In February 2002, one of Tookagain's B.A. students, Monalisa DaVinci, submitted an untitled short story to him as a required component of the course. Professor Tookagain made a number of typographical and grammatical corrections to Monalisa's story, along with some written suggestions regarding characterisation and plot development. Tookagain remarked that Monalisa's heroine needed to be in a love triangle and that her character should be more dramatic, 'without necessarily saying much'. He suggested *The Puzzling Smile* as a possible title. Monalisa adopted Professor Tookagain's corrections in full and rewrote her story in line with his suggestions before resubmitting it under the title of *The Intriguing Smile*. (Tookagain's students were not required to hand in drafts but were encouraged to do so if they wanted additional feedback.) She received an "A" grade on her 20-page paper.

2001 had been a bad year for Professor Tookagain. He had had a prolonged bout of "writer's block" and had written barely a line of fiction. One evening during the 2002 Easter vacation, while relaxing at home after a light supper, he decided to leaf through some of the short stories submitted by his students to try to get his creative juices flowing again. Tookagain reread Monalisa's short story several times and made some notes from it. The next evening he went to his office at the University and, using his computer (supplied to him by his department as part of his job), Tookagain started writing a novel about a dramatic heroine called Monalisa, who is coveted by two lovers and cannot decide which to choose. A furious bout with his computer over that week saw the work completed in just 7 days. (The fastest Tookagain had ever taken previously to complete a novel was 6 months.) Tookagain's regular publisher quickly accepted the manuscript and *The Smile that Intrigues* was published in paperback as "Another brilliant story from the pen of J. R. Tookagain". The 200-page book contained no acknowledgements. It took off to become an international best-seller.

In November 2002, Lion Productions, a Hollywood studio, approached Tookagain to buy the film rights to the book. Tookagain agreed to license them in return for a percentage based on booking office receipts and for royalties on video and DVD sales. The film was released in September 2003 as *The Smile That Kills* and was an instant success. Tookagain became a millionaire overnight.

One of Monalisa's fellow creative writing students saw *The Smile That Kills* and thought it resembled the plot of Monalisa's short story, which she had shown him sometime in 2002 after receiving her grade. He spoke to Monalisa, who went to see the film. She was shocked and appalled to find that what appeared to be "her" story was there on the screen without her consent, billed moreover as a work "based on *The Smile That Intrigues* by J.R. Tookagain". Having now read Tookagain's novel for the first time at the library, she formed the view that it was just an expanded version of her short story. When approached, Professor Tookagain replied that "ideas are free as the air" and denied he had taken her story.

Monalisa, who has been struggling to get by on her student loan, instructed solicitors to issue proceedings on her behalf against Tookagain. She claimed a declaration that she was the true author of *The Smile That Intrigues,* that Professor Tookagain had infringed her copyright, and that he had also acted in breach of confidence. The question of relief was left over for decision after judgment on liability.

The University of Erewhon also issued proceedings, claiming a declaration that it owned the copyright in *The Smile That Intrigues* and that it was therefore entitled to the proceeds from the book and the film. According to the University, the story had been written in the course of the professor's employment with it, and that, under the University's statutes (which were conceded to be binding on Tookagain), it owned copyright 'in works generated by computer hardware or software owned or operated by the University'. Uncontradicted evidence from Professor Tookagain and other academic staff at the university establishes, however, a long-held general understanding that academic staff owned copyright in any books or articles they produce. It is also accepted that students at the University of Erewhon own the copyright in any material they submit for course work.

After hearing the parties, the High Court of Erewhon, affirmed by the Erewhon Court of Appeal, issued a final judgment declaring that:-

1 Professor Tookagain owed no duty of confidence to Monalisa in respect of *The Intriguing Smile* short story.

2 The underlying idea of *The Intriguing Smile* was not original and was not therefore protected by copyright.

3 Even if *The Intriguing Smile* were considered original, Monalisa had no right to be recognised as the author of the book *The Smile That Intrigues* because the crux of the plot of both works had come from Professor Tookagain and had been merely adopted by her when she rewrote her draft for him.

4 Whatever copyright existed in the novel belonged to the University of Erewhon as a "work generated by computer hardware or software owned…by the University" by Professor Tookagain in the course of his employment, and the University was therefore entitled to the copyright in *The Smile That Intrigues* and to the proceeds from the book and the resulting film.

After the Court of Appeal hearing, the University and Monalisa settled their differences with the University agreeing to share whatever proceeds it received from the book and film with Monalisa equally. It would however leave Monalisa free to make whatever arguments she chose on appeal, and would abide by any final decision on copyright and entitlement. The University further agrees to abide by the settlement with Monalisa even if the Supreme Court upholds the fourth declaration in its favour. Tookagain was advised of this settlement and instructed his lawyers not to challenge its validity.

Monalisa has appealed to the Supreme Court of Erewhon, and has asked the Court to reverse all four declarations made by the High Court, and to substitute declarations in her favour. Alternatively, if in considering the case on the fourth declaration, the Court concludes that Monalisa is not the beneficial owner of the copyright in the book and no declaration in her favour should be made, Monalisa seeks to uphold the declaration in favour of the University. Tookagain cross-appeals the declaration made in favour of the University. The Court has accepted the University's request that it take no part in the hearing on its undertaking to be bound by the judgment of the Court.

Having lost all its jurisprudence in the great flood of Erewhon, the Supreme Court will accept arguments based on precedents and statute law from other jurisdictions as persuasive authority. Ultimately, however, it will make its decision in law on the basis of principle.

CASE FOR THE APPELLANT—In Favour of Monalisa.

This case seems complex on the surface but it can be broken down and systematically analysed. Monalisa DaVinci has begun with the creation of a draft essay, handed in to Professor Tookagain to be assessed. She subsequently takes his suggestions and merges the collection of ideas to produce the essay "The intriguing smile". Therefore part of the idea came from Professor Tookagain, but it was Monalisa who brought the various strands together to produce the essay submission which has now been fixed in copyright in the form of her essay.

It was stated in the case University of London Press Ltd v University Tutorial Press Ltd[1] that "*Copyright acts not concerned with the originality of ideas but with the expression of thought, and in the case of 'literary work', with the expression of thought in print or writing*".

Monalisa submitted a draft essay.

Professor Tookagain made some vague suggestions such as that a character should be more dramatic or a love triangle.

These suggested situations are so much in the public domain that they are found in every other book or film and they are so vague that surely Professor Tookagain cannot entertain the idea that he provided the crux of Monalisa's essay "*The intriguing smile*".

Monalisa took all of the ideas, developed and intertwined all of them together, elaborating them as in the case of Roth Greeting Cards v United Card Co.[2], where the judge said "*In order to be copyrightable, the work must be the original work of the copyright claimant or of his predecessor in interest. But the originality necessary to support a copyright merely calls for independent creation, not novelty.*"

Therefore, Monalisa took several ideas and by using them in her draft essay, she produced the independent creation subsequently fixated as "*The intriguing smile*".

---

1   University of London Press Ltd v University Tutorial Press Ltd [1916] 2 Ch 601 at 608.
2   Roth Greeting Cards v United Card Co. [1970] US

Plagiarism

The essence of Monalisa's claim is that Professor Tookagain has stolen and plagiarised the work of Monalisa Da Vinci to put together his novel. Plagiarism is identified by the following two-stage procedure:

1   Access—this is easily determined by the availability and admittance of Professor Tookagain that he read "The intriguing smile" several times.

2   Substantial similarity. The test for substantial similarity is more difficult to quantify. The test is outlined in the case of Roth Greeting Cards v United Card Co. and the judgement states: "*The test of infringement is whether the work is recognisable by an ordinary observer as having been taken from the copyrighted source*".

This is plain to see because a third party, a fellow creative writer student, recognised Monalisa" story in the movie portrayal of Professor Tookagain" book. It is clear that Professor Tookagain has copied the fixated form of Monalisa's essay. The facts show that—

-   Monalisa made a copyrightable essay submission;

-   The lecturer and famous author Professor Tookagain who was suffering from a period of writers' block must have been under enormous pressure, frustration and fear of failure.

-   That one day he comes to see a Grade A Paper and reads it several times and then begins to write. At this stage his ownership of the original work does not give him ownership of copyright.

-   He completes writing a novel in seven days where-as he previously would have taken six months./

-   His novel is substantially similar and recognisable to the essay written by Monalisa in the eyes of any reasonable man;

-   This is clearly a breach of copyright;

-   Professor Tookagain renamed, repackaged and relied on a few minor alterations to the intriguing smile and stole and used Monalisa's story as the kernel for a 200 page elaboration of the short story know as "*The smile that intrigues*";

-   The protection of the rights of unknown authors is essential to ensure the maintenance of a high level of creativity in the literary world;

Therefore, we ask the Court to recognise that Professor Tookagain did in fact owe a duty of confidence to one of his students, Monalisa Da Vinci.

We also ask the Court to recognise the ownership of copyright towards Monalisa Da Vinci of the short story she wrote "*The intriguing smile*" and that Professor Tookagain has committed a breach of the copyright through the publication of his novel "*The smile that intrigues*".

As to the University's rights of authorship, we remind the Court that Professor Tookagain is bound by University Statute and that it is a long-standing tradition that students own copyright in any material they submit for coursework.

THE CASE FOR THE RESPONDENT—Professor Tookagain

Subsistence is of copyright issue. It is on subsistence that the underlying idea of "The intriguing smile" relies to assert that copyright does not belong to Monalisa, the Appellant. The Appellant merely adopted the Professor's ideas. What the Professor has taken is the underlying idea. The question is whether copyright exists in the idea. English law takes the view that copyright does not extend to ideas.

The principle justification of our case lies in the Treaties. Also, Article 1 of the United States Constitution states that "…progress of science and literary works by protecting ideas.,.." So, if mere ideas are protected, this gives the first writer and the first painter, copyright protection and this would stifle the expression of others.

If we look at the facts in the Monalisa story, we do not even know the name that Monalisa gave to her heroine. The Professor did not take that name—he took Monalisa's name. There are many works which are unique and are based on ideas of previous works.

Also, in the French raconteur system, copyright may protect underlying ideas. In English law, the threshold level for copyright is set very low. [3]

We submit that Monalisa's work has no spark of originality.

Breach of Confidence

The essay for which confidence is claimed is not of the nature of confidentiality.

The Professor has not breached the duty of confidentiality even if there was confidentiality.[4] In the Amway case, duty of confidence attached from a large body of know-how gleaned from conversations, extensive literature, etc. But information standing alone cannot be a breach of confidence.

We submit that the sole source of Monalisa's information was from professor Tookagain. Even if Monalisa had some ideas, this would not attach a duty of confidence to the whole book as in the Amway case.

---

3   See the case University of London Press
4   See the Amway Corporation case.

Copyright

Monalisa would find it difficult to establish copyright in the Professor's book because she did not write it but she seeks to prove that copyright subsists to the University[5].

In the Stevenson case, the matter was regarding a managing consultant who had prepared a book, part of which was contained in the Work's Manuals and part of which consisted of lectures which he gave at work.

The business test is to establish that the Professor's work is part of the University. A long-held understanding as to published works by lecturers is not an express agreement. Express terms of the statute say to the contrary. In the case of Knower v Shiva, they were able to establish that a long-held understanding can be taken as a term of contract. But this case is unlike Knower v Shiva in that the University has express terms to the contrary.

The Judges' Decision

Right Honourable Justice Jacobs and Justice Mummery

The Court of Appeal states that there is no copyright in the part of the student's work which was taken by Professor Tookagain.

The Court of Appeal found no fact on infringement because the Court of appeal found no copyright in the essay.

As to Breach of Confidence, Justice Jacob said that the essay is fiction. Justice Mummery said that the manuscript is information. The essay had the limited purpose of grading the student's work. The Professor used the notes he made of the text. He did not use the text of the essay.

Justice Mummery said that the abuse of confidence is an equitable doctrine.

On this Appeal, Monalisa, who is the claimant in these proceedings, challenges the Court of Appeal findings. There are two disputes: non-copyright dispute and the ideas in the book and film. Monalisa asserts that the book is taken from her short story.

1   The Professor was under a duty not to use the manuscript by Monalisa save as to purpose of the writing course. The Professor is not able to use covertly and clandestinely Monalisa'a work.

---

5   See the Stevenson, Jordan case

2   The second decision astonishingly contains a *non-sequitor*. The real question raised and not addressed is whether copyright exists in the original short story. It is protected by copyright. We set aside the Higher Court's decision and say that copyright subsists.

3   Does Monalisa have the right to be the author of the novel because her short story and the novel had the same crux? We say that the novel has ideas in the form of plot and characterisation and that Monalisa has no right to be the author of the novel simply because her ideas were used. Although there was collaboration of a kind between Monalisa and the Professor, there was no collaboration in the novel. Therefore Monalisa had no right to be recognised as author of the book.

4   We say the source of the plot may be relevant to the question of infringement but these are not matters which this court can decide. So far as infringement is concerned, this will have to be remitted to a lower court.

5   Finally, we say that the University is not entitled to the proceeds of the book or film. We say that copyright does not belong to the University. The Professor did not write his novel as part of the course of teaching creative writing. He is already an established writer. All he has done is use the computer equipment. Therefore "generated by computer hardware" does not apply.

2004 MOCK TRIAL—
On-Line Publishing Issues
(full transcript)

Who controls The On-Line Distribution of Newspaper Articles? Author or publisher?

This Mock Trial was between Julian Putney Claimant and Peachy Universe Inc, Defendant. The claimant is an international freelance author of newspaper and magazine articles and the sole author of hundreds of original literary works in the form of articles he has written for various print publications including newspapers, magazines and other paper-based forms in the UK since the 1970's. The defendant is a global media conglomerate incorporated under the laws of the United states, and prints and publishes the newspaper "The Peach" among many others. The claimant is the owner of the copyright in a number of articles submitted to the defendant for publication in its newspaper "The Peach" only. The Claimant states that he did not licence or assign the defendant the right to copy, produce, reproduce, communicate, disseminate or publish the Works in any electronic media and that the defendant has infringed his copyright through electronic means. One of the works was titled "Do I dare eat a peach?" and that the reproduced Works are a derogatory treatment of the Claimant's works because the Works appeared alongside an advertisement for an on-line gambling game run by "The Peach" entitled Peachy.Gambling.com and an advertisement for "PeachyGirls.com", a pornographic site. The Claimant seeks an injunction restraining the defendant from infringing his copyright and an order to deliver up all articles in the defendant's possession belonging to the defendant and damages and costs.

Julian Putney, played by Mr Benet Brandreth
Defendant's managing editor, played by Mr Harry Small
Claimant's counsel. played by Mr Henry Carr, QC

Defendant's counsel, played by Mr Michael Silverleaf QC
Judge, played by Mr Christopher Floyd QC.

Claimant's Counsel, Mr Carr QC: The Claimant is a well-known free-lance author. One of his articles is "Do I dare eat a peach?". This article is about consuming large quantities of fruit. It is about whether you should eat a peach after other fruit has been consumed.

In 1973, Mr Putney's article was published by "The Peach".

In 1977 certain works, including "Do I dare eat a peach?" were put into electronic form and the public who subscribe can download these articles.

The issues are: Is there a freezing act in the UK? The host is based in Florida. The articles were copied there. The public are encouraged to download these articles. The public includes users of "The Peach" in the UK. The claimant says that this represents and amounts to an infringement of his copyright.

Judge: When does this infringement occur?

Claimant's Counsel: It occurs when article is downloaded. Mr Putney consented to the publication of his work in 'The Peach'. He received a one-off payment of £20. There is no suggestion that he received any more money. The Defendant claims that Mr Putney put no restrictions on whether his articles could be published. Mr Putney gave consent to publish in print, in the newspaper and no more. Therefore consent is implied; it is an implied licence by silence as per contract law. Phillips Electronics v BskyB is the well known principle in respect of implied terms.

Carr: But in Robin Ray v Classic FM, Classic FM had sold the foreign rights abroad. This is implied licence. Only implication is minimum necessary.

Judge: The more implied the contract, the less room there is for the court to imply.

Carr: Therefore that is not a warrant for implying more than the parties had agreed at the stage. The case the defendant has to satisfy is that Mr Putnam will have inevitably said "yes"—for no more money.

There is express consent in 1977.

It is implied. Mr Putney found out that his article was on-line in 2002. The action commenced with no positive act of encouragement. The defendant has to prove some positive act amounting to consent. Furthermore, there is derogatory treatment of Mr Putney's article because it is on-line in association with a gambling pop-up and a pornography advert. Mr Putney has moral rights—rights to object to the derogatory treatment of his work. In the present case, the work is in electronic version; the reader sees a pop-up gambling advert. This is no co-incidence. There is a hyperlink involved. Mr Putney has a public stance against gambling. It is a well known public stance. And matters are not helped by the link to the porn site. The legal issue is—does this fall within the definition of 'treatment' in the Act? The relevant words here are 'in addition to'. This means adding text. For example, assume that the work is published in conjunction with Nazi memorabilia, for example. It would be detrimental to the work, for example, if the work was about the Holocaust. So the work becomes derogated by the treatment. 'Capable of treatment' includes additions which is the association which is detrimental to the work.

Judge: So the reader does not need to come to the conclusion that it is part of the work. If he does, then it is part of the work.

CALLED FIRST WITNESS MR PUTNEY.

Mr Silverleaf QC: Mr Putney, you are a well-known author, aren't you?

Mr Putney: I like to feel so.

Mr Silverleaf QC: You graduated in 1977 and you researched your article about a peach for three years?

Mr Putney: Yes.

Mr Silverleaf QC: This was your first significant publication. You did not have a previous publication. And a number of publications had rejected this article, did they not?

Mr Putney: True. That was their loss.

Mr Silverleaf: It took some time to persuade 'Peach' newspaper to take your work, did it not? You approached 'Peach' to try and persuade them to publish it?

Mr Putney: Yes.

Mr Silverleaf: You simply asked 'Peach' to publish and they agreed?

Mr Putney: Yes.

Mr Silverleaf: There was no written agreement at the time of publication?

Mr Putney: No. Why?

Mr Silverleaf: Had it been re-published, you would have been pleased, wouldn't you?

Mr Putney: Yes. But if it were to be re-published by "Hustler" for example, I would say no. If the "New Statesman" wanted to publish it, I would say, yes.

Mr. Silverleaf: The more you are published, the more you become known, isn't that so?

Mr Putney: But I do not want it read by the Hoi Poloi.

Mr Silverleaf: You are aware that "Peach" keeps an archive and that this archive is available for consultation by writers, are you not?

Mr Putney: Yes, possibly.

Mr Silverleaf: Your article is available from "Peach"s archive, isn't it? And the archive is held on microfiche, isn't it?

Mr Putney: I assumed that they only held the original copies.

Mr Silverleaf: So you had no objection to your article being on the archive?

Mr Putney: No. In the sense that Peach was retaining old copies for research purposes.

Mr Silverleaf: The availability of the article on-line increases its publicity. If accessed by the public, they are likely to read your work and this would enhance your reputation, wouldn't it?

Mr Putney: Yes.

Mr Silverleaf: This is in fact Peach's electronic archive, accessible on-line. This is exactly the same in kind as a microfiche archive, isn't it?

Mr Putney: No. This one can be taken down and thrown about.

Mr Silverleaf: The only difference is that it is accessed on computer instead of microfiche, isn't it?

Mr Putney.: No. When it is accessed on computer, it is published again and again. Certainly there are no casinos or table-dancing in the microfiche archive as there are on computer.

Mr Silverleaf: You don't like table-dancing, do you?

Mr Putney: No

Mr Silverleaf: You were invited to Miami to a party to launch Peach's online archive, weren't you?

Mr Putney: Yes.

Mr Silverleaf: The invitation told you that the party was to launch the electronic archive, didn't it?

Mr Putney: Yes. I was sent an aero-plane ticket to Miami.

Mr Silverleaf: So you knew about the on-line version "Peachy", didn't you?

Mr. Putney: Yes.

Mr Silverleaf: You didn't suggest to other guests that they were including your work in their archive?

Mr Putney: No. I assumed they would ask me to re-publish my article and that I would be offered more money.

Mr Silverleaf: So it was just a question of money, was it?

Mr Putney: Yes.

Mr Silverleaf: You carried out a 'Google' search and found your article, didn't you?

Mr Putney: Yes.

Mr Silverleaf: You use a computer and you are aware that all newspapers follow that trend and publish on-line, aren't you?

Mr Putney: I do not follow the history of the internet.

Mr Silverleaf: I assume that you know that your work would appear there?

Mr Putney: I would have agreed if they had offered me some more cash.

Mr Silverleaf: But you were invited to the party?

Mr Putney: Yes.

Mr Silverleaf: You have a strong aversion to gambling, don't you?

Mr Putney: I've had a very bad experience.

Mr Silverleaf: But the majority of people have no objection to gambling, do they?

Mr Putney: I object.

Mr Silverleaf: You also object to the porn sites, do you?

Mr Putney: Yes, very much.

Mr Silverleaf: But you do understand that Peach has no control of other internet Pop-ups?

Mr Putney: So you say.

Mr Silverleaf: Was your article on-line word-for-word as it was first published, with nothing added or taken away from it?

Mr Putney: Yes.

Mr Silverleaf: You accessed the Peach website. Did you not have to register to access it?

Mr Putney: Yes.

Mr Silverleaf: There was a registration process. You have to enter your name, address, etc.

Mr Putney: Yes, but you can put in anything.

Mr Silverleaf: But you put in a false name and false address, didn't you?

Mr Putney: Yes, you couldn't get access to it otherwise.

Mr Silverleaf: No more questions, My Lord.

WITNESS—managing director of newspaper PEACH called, Mr Orchard Bloom.

Mr CARR QC Mr Bloom, can you confirm that that is your witness statement before you?

Mr Bloom: It is.

Mr Carr: It mentions that you joined PEACH newspaper in 1971 and that you became Managing Director in 1977. Was it your idea to have the on-line archive?

Mr Bloom: Yes.

Mr Carr: You are pleased with the web-site. Does it make a profit?

Mr Bloom: Yes, an indirect profit.

Mr Carr: PEACHES on-line gambling site is also doing very well. The idea is to advertise the gambling site, isn't it?

Mr Bloom: Yes.

Mr Carr: When did you find out about Mr Putney's query?

Mr Bloom: When the action came to light.

Mr Carr: But Mr Putney abhors gambling, doesn't he?

Mr Bloom: Mr Putney has strong views about everything. He has a strong ego. In fact PEACH GIRLS.com, the table-dancing web-site would use web-crawlers to capture the public who link to my web-site. But pop-ups can be disabled, Mr Carr.

Mr Carr: Does the connection with PEACHY GIRLS not distress you, Mr Bloom?

Mr Bloom: No. Only if you couldn't get rid of it.

Mr Carr: But you have a strong interest in pornography, do you not, Mr Bloom?

Mr Bloom:: Oh, that!

Mr Carr: Do you edit that as well?

Mr Bloom: I like to keep abreast of what's going on!

Mr Carr: But the Peach newspaper Board regarded that connection to the porn web-site as a bit dodgy, didn't they?

Mr Bloom: Yes, I had to convince the Board otherwise.

Mr Carr: You would have had to ask the authors' consent, wouldn't you?

Mr Bloom: I find that most authors are like children when it comes to business.

Mr Carr: So did you raise the question to the Board of whether you needed the authors' consent?

Mr Bloom: No.

Mr Carr: In the mid-1990's, you began to circulate bulletins, didn't you?

Mr Bloom: The Bulletins were not to notify but to remind them.

Mr Carr: So, even people who consented since 1973 would know about your planned on-line archive?

Mr Bloom: The matter is about work being permanently recorded. It is published so it is permanently recorded.

Mr Carr: Was Mr Putney sent one of these notices? How do you know that he was sent one?

Mr Bloom: His name is on a database. All persons on the database were sent a notice. Therefore he received a notice in the mid-1990's.

Mr Carr: Why did you bother to send out a notice? You sent it out because you were conscious that to go on-line, you would need the author's consent, weren't you?

In the 1970's, it was not even in the author's imagination that it would become possible to publish on the internet, was it?

Mr Bloom: Yes.

Mr Carr: You know Mr Putney very well. So when you decided to publish his work, why didn't you just call and ask for his consent?

Mr Bloom: There was no legal requirement. I don't think he would have said "no". His ego would have wanted it to be published.

Mr Carr: But you must have been aware of that risk?

Mr Bloom: No.

Mr Carr: But you intended that Mr Putney would attend the launch party and you mentioned that at the launch party he appeared drunk and emotional, didn't you?

Mr Bloom: The party was to celebrate the publishing on the web-site. I inferred from his demented behaviour that he was clearly happy about something. On the occasion of the celebration party in Miami, he was happy because his ego had been given a boost because of the on-line archive.

Mr Carr: You claim that you can only get on-line by entering a valid United States Zip Code only. If you put in a UK post-code, you can still subscribe, isn't that true?

Mr Bloom: We limited access to US citizens only. It was a marketing decision in 1997 to introduce access region by region.

Mr Carr: We are now in 2004. Have you progressed?

Mr Bloom: Yes.

Mr Carr: Last Monday, you carried UK cricket scores on your on-line web-site. Why did you do that if access is only to US citizens?

Mr Bloom: There are many 'Brits' in the US.

Mr Carr: No further questions, My Lord.

ADDRESSES TO THE COURT

By Mr Silverleaf, QC-representing the Defendant Newspaper:

There are four issues here.

Infringement. By common consent, there is no reproduction by my client in the UK. There is copying by electronic form by subscribers through their computers. Infringement requires presentation in numbers designed to indicate that the user is allowed to access work. But access to the work is only in the US. There is no authorisation to access the work in the UK. Accordingly, access from the UK is not authorised by my client and therefore there is no infringement.

Consent. There are two questions in relation to consent. Was there express consent and was there original consent? Mr Putney was very keen to publish his work in 1973 and there was consent to publication without limitation.

There was no written agreement and no terms were agreed. The PEACH newspaper has always published material archived after publication. Therefore the terms which should be implied when no terms are agreed are that no restrictions are imposed.

This must be so, otherwise, every time that my client wished to organise his business in a particular way, he would have to ask consent.

Judge: But your client did send out a bulletin. Why did the bulletin not say "Please confirm your consent"?

Mr Silverleaf QC: The notice of the bulletin is a clear indication that there was consent. The matter was put beyond doubt by the 1997 Miami party to celebrate the on-line web-site. Mr Putney was invited as one of the authors.

My Lord, you should wholly reject his claim.

Judge: But he was not told that his article would appear in the archive on-line, was he?

Mr Silverleaf QC: It is the smallest possible step for him to understand that his writings were included. His conduct at the party was inconsistent with the notion that he did not consent.

The third issue I raise is that of ESTOPPEL because of derogatory treatment of Mr Putney's work. I say that it's not treatment to put pop-ups of gambling and porn on the same web-site and in any event it is not derogatory. The matters of consent are not because there were additions to his work; the pop-ups are clearly separate. The remedy must lie in defamation. He has no remedy in copyright.

Judge: But the pop-ups could imply "look how idiotic this article is!".

Mr Silverleaf QC: Mr Putney is not being deprived of a remedy. But there is no remedy in copyright.

Judge: But remedies can overlap.

Mr Silverleaf QC: But not in this case. The Court is not bothered by the author's reaction to the pop-ups but to the public reaction. It is simply not possible to say that the general public will treat the pop-ups as capable of having a connection. My Lord, we ask you to dismiss the action.

Mr. Carr-Representing the Claimant author Mr Putney: The first issue—what is the relevance of the certification system in the US? We say, it makes no difference. We say that the idea that gradual introduction by region must have expired after 6 years since 1996. Also, neither the subscriber nor the recipient cares about this. If you divorce the question of authorisation to access the website from the question of certification, there is no relevance.

As to the Defendant's argument that silence amounts to express consent, we say that that is rubbish. There are many ways of contracting authors. The reason why Mr Bloom did not contact the authors to get their consent is he found the Board difficult and he thought that the authors might be difficult also. His bulletin was asserted as ex post facto consent in that if you did not disapprove links, you consented.

The evidence shows that both Mr Bloom and Mr Putney were drunk at the Miami party. There is no suggestion that at the party Mr Putney was told that his work would be on-line. His concern now is genuine. If he is genuinely concerned now, why did he consent then in 1997 at the party?

As to the matter of derogatory treatment, all that matters is whether something has been added. There is the purpose to giving moral right.

Further there is no remedy in defamation. It is not defamatory to make fun of the author. If we look at the treatment of Mr Putney's work on-line objectively, we see that whether derogatory or not, the links to the subject of gambling and pornography are there. Viewers are supposed to appreciate the links and assume that the author has consented to the links.

JUDGEMENT

Judge: In this case, the treatment of the work was taken as the work itself. So we say that the problem is one of association. Mr Putney has taken a public stance against gambling and the same is true of the pornographic web-site.

In this action, Mr Putney claims damages for infringement of copyright and moral right. The Defendant publishes a newspaper called PEACH and PEACHYINFO ON_LINE.

The dispute centers on the fact that Mr Putney discovered his article "Do I dare eat a peach?" on-line. He claims that as it occurs in the UK, it is a breach of his copyright.

The questions to be answered are:

1   Has the Defendant authorised publication in the UK, given that the web-site operated in the US?

2   Has publication been expressly given by Mr Putney or is there an implied consent?

3   Is this a matter for estoppel?

4   Is there a breach of Mr Putney's moral rights as per Copyright Act 1988?

In order to access the article from the web-site, anybody who wishes to read it can register. The subscriber has to give US details. In the course of the evidence we heard that this restriction was due to a marketing decision in 1997 for business purposes. So, have the defendants authorised publication in the UK? A subscriber had to certify that he was from the US. But a US person can download the article on a computer in the UK. Therefore I UPHOLD that the defendants authorised the downloading from the UK.

As to the express or implied consent due to Mr Putney's consent for publication in 1973: I say that mere silence is NOT express licence to use the article as the defendant sees fit. Nor is it necessary to imply a licence for electronic use. Such an implied licence is only permissible on the usual grounds of terms of a contract.

In 1973, when the article was first published, the internet had not been invented. Nobody could have foreseen the internet. Therefore there is no necessary implication of the right to use the article in electronic form.

As to the factual dispute. Mr Putney and Mr Bloom both tended to remember matters as they would like them to be. Mr Putney struck me as a flamboyant egoist and Mr Bloom as a shrewd businessman. The defendant intended to launch the electronic publication of PEACH. In my judgement this does not amount to express consent to use Mr Putney" articles. Nor should Mr Putney be estopped from complaining about the use of his article.

There has been an infringement of the Copyright Act 1988. There was no express or implied consent. There was no derogatory treatment of the article. The statutory right (section 80) is to object to the treatment of work published in a derogatory manner. Mr Carr focussed on the words "in addition to". In my judgement, it is not the case here that the pop-ups have any reference to the work. The pop-ups cannot amount to derogatory treatment. Mr Carr's examples may indeed amount to derogatory treatment but NOT in this case.

No permission to appeal is given.

2003 IP MOOT—An ex-addict's published article revealed after 20 years (the facts)

FACT SITUATION

INTERNATIONAL INTELLECTUAL PROPERTY LAW MOOT 2003

Addicts United ("AU") is a non-profit support group in Erewhon for recovering drug and drinking addicts. It circulates a newsletter entitled "For You Only" among its current members, in which members exchange success stories to encourage one another in recovery. AU's secretary occasionally sends current copies of the newsletter to the public library in the town where she lives, although the AU executive and membership have not been informed and does not know of this fact.

In 1980 Marco Polo, then a university student, joined AU to help in his recovery from what his medical practitioner had diagnosed as incipient alcoholism. The programme proved successful and, at the suggestion of his recovery group leader, Polo wrote an account of his history with drink and how AU had helped him, and sent this account to the editor of "For You Only". Polo was confident that his article would be beneficial to the readership of "For You Only" and did not expect or receive any payment from AU for the piece. The article duly appeared in a 1980 issue of the newsletter.

In 2002, Polo decided to run for Parliament. A persuasive and charismatic speaker, he has been steadily gaining support within his proposed constituency for his platform of zero tolerance of drugs, prohibition of alcohol, and automatic custodial sentences for drink-driving and drug offences.

In the middle of his campaign, Polo was contacted by a friend, who told him that Polo's AU article appeared on a website called 'Beforetheywerefamous.co.erewhon' which was operated by Devil-May-Care Internet Co. Ltd. in Erewhon. This site, as its name suggests, runs items about celebrities, particularly about what they did before gaining fame. It appears that the article was obtained from a copy of the newsletter sent in 1980 by AU's secretary to her local public library.

Shocked and appalled, Polo sought an immediate temporary injunction against Devil-May-Care Internet Co. Ltd. to remove the article from the website. He claimed that the continuing appearance of the article on the website infringed his copyright and right of privacy, and was a breach of confidence.

The High Court of Erewhon, affirmed by the Court of Appeal, dismissed Polo's claim, holding:

a) There was no infringement of copyright because Polo had, by his consent to the publication and circulation of the article in "For You Only", impliedly licensed his article to be displayed on the website;

b) There was no breach of confidence because the article's appearance in "For You Only" and in the public library rendered the information no longer confidential;

c) There was no "right of privacy" in Erewhon's law;

d) The website's activities were protected by Article 10 of the European Convention on Human Rights guaranteeing freedom of expression.[6]

Polo has appealed to the Supreme Court of Erewhon, and has asked that Court reverse all four holdings of the lower courts. After having lost all jurisprudence of its own to the great fire of Erewhon, the Supreme Court will accept arguments based on precedents and statute law from other jurisdictions as persuasive authority. However, it will ultimately make its decision of law on the basis of principle.

---

6   While the Convention has not been formally incorporated into Erewhon's law, Erewhon's courts, including the Supreme Court, have declared that they would normally treat the Convention's provisions as part of the law of Erewhon.

2003 IP MOOT (example 1—appellant's case)

<u>IN THE SUPREME COURT</u>   Case No. 2003 POLO 0001

BETWEEN
MARCO POLO
       <u>Claimant</u>
       and

DEVIL-MAY-CARE INTERNET COMPANY LIMITED   <u>Defendant</u>

3.   <u>Introduction</u>

3.1 This is an application on appeal from the Court of Appeal, on behalf of the Claimant, for an immediate interim injunction to restrain the defendants from printing, publishing, selling or otherwise circulating an article which it is claimed is infringing the copyright of the claimant.

3.2 The application is made to remove an article written by the Claimant (C) from the Defendant's website 'Beforetheywerefamous.co.erewhon' and to restrain the Defendant (D) from further publication and infringement of copyright in the article, breach of confidence and breach of privacy. The Claimant (C) disputes the finding that the granting of an interim injunction in this matter would breach Article 10 of the European Convention on Human Rights (ECHR)which guarantees freedom of expression.

4.   <u>Background</u>

4.1 In 1980, the Claimant, then a student, suffered from an alcohol-related disorder and after treatment and the assistance of 'Addicts United', he wrote a personal account of his experience and recovery and sent the article to the editor of 'For You Only' (FYO) newsletter. The FYO newsletter is an in-house newsletter of the Erewon non-profit support group 'Addicts United' (AU) and is distributed to members of the group. AU's work is to support recovering drug and alcohol addicts. The article was duly published in the FYO newsletter issued in 1980.

4.2 In an unauthorised act, the secretary of FYO sent the newsletter to her local public library, from which the Defendant, Devil-May-Care Internet Company Limited (DMCI), twenty-two years later, in 2002, obtained a copy and placed it on their web-site which runs articles about celebrities' lives before they gained public prominence.

5. Argument

The argument is based on the following submissions:

5.1 Copyright in the article has been breached.

5.2 There has been a breach of confidence by publication by DCMI of the newsletter on the world-wide web and thus the public domain.

5.3 When there is copyright material which was not intended for wider publication, there is a right to privacy of information.

5.4 Article 10(2)ECHR applies as there is an interference with the right of the Claimant

5.5 Whether granting an immediate interim injunction is appropriate.

6. Argument 3.1.: Copyright in the article has been breached.

C did not make any arrangement for a public lending right in his work. C did not expect that the article would be circulated beyond the readership of FYO. Therefore he did not grant a universal licence of his work to all who might wish to copy his article. Even if there had been a public lending right, this did not authorise infringement of C's copyright or that of the licence holder of the copyright subsisting in the article The court is asked to examine the Berne Convention of 1886 and 1971 in this matter.

Further, it was incumbent on D to establish the ownership of the copyright and its subsistence prior to publication, which D failed to do. There is no implied licence from this unauthorised publication on the internet. Also, D copied the full article onto his website, in contravention of the Copyright, Design and Patents Act 1988 (UK). This is not fair dealing., nor is it in the public interest to have C's article on DMCI's website. This is supported by a summary of fair dealing by Sir Andrew Morritt as stated in paragraph 70 the case of *Ashdown v Sunday Telegraph Group Ltd EWCA Civ 1142, [2002] QB 546* and states

"It is impossible to lay down any hard-and-fast definition of what is fair dealing, for it is matter of fact, degree and impression. However, by far the most important factor is whether the alleged fair dealing is in fact commercially competing with the proprietor" exploitation of the copyright work, a substitute for the probable purchase of authorised copies, and the like…The second most important factor is whether the work has already been published or otherwise exposed to the public. If it has not, and especially if the material has been obtained by a breach of confidence or other means or underhand dealing, the courts will be reluctant to say it is fair…."

To permit the continued publication on the internet would be to deprive the copyright owner, C, of the right which statute has guaranteed. DCMI cannot claim that the article was put on the internet for the purpose of review because DCMI did not review the twenty two year old article on their web-site.

Argument 3.2: There has been a breach of confidence by DCMI

As in the case of *Coco v AN Clark [1969] RPC 41*, it is submitted that the information in the Claimant's article contains information which in itself is of a confidential character. Also, the case of *Naomi Campbell v MGN [2002] EWCA 1373*, it was held that in order to establish a claim for breach of confidence, three matters had to be established:

1.   that the details published had "the necessary quality of confidence" about them;

2.   that the details were imparted in circumstances importing an obligation of confidence and

3.   that the publication of the details was to the plaintiff's detriment.

The first test was the requirement that disclosure or observation of information would be highly offensive to a reasonable person of ordinary sensibilities as in the case of *Australian Broadcasting Corp v Lench Game Meats [2001] HCA 63* To read about a past illness of this respectable claimant is shocking.

The second test comes from Lord Woolf CJ judgement in *A v B [2002] EWCA Civ 337*, in which he said "…usually the answer to the question whether there exists a private interest worthy of protection will be obvious". It is submitted that there is a private interest worthy of protection from information regarding alcoholism twenty two years earlier.

This third test is fulfilled ; it is clear that C would not have authorised the internet display of his article by DMCI…

Since there is the absence of a fiduciary relationship between C and DMCI, there is a claim for breach of confidence and unlawful interference as in the case of *Indata Equipment Supplies Ltd (Trading as Autofleet) v ACL Ltd [1998] FSR 248.*

Argument 3.3: There is a right of privacy of information in article

The Court is asked to have regard to the case of *Douglas & Hello v OK Magazine [2001] FSR 732* in which the judges were unanimous in calling for a right to privacy.

Article 8 UK Human Rights Act, Right to Privacy, should hold as Polo legitimately chose to keep this matter private and it is not topical.

The judgement in *A v B [2002] EWCA Civ 337*, at paragraph 48 states "..Where an individual is a public figure, he is entitled to have his privacy respected in the appropriate circumstances, A public figure is entitled to a private life…."

The court should also look at how the matter is treated in different countries. In Germany and France, it is an actionable wrong to publish without consent.

In Canada, the Quebec Charter states in its Provision 5: "Every person has a right to respect for his private life". This is the same privacy right as in Article 12 of the Universal Declaration of Human Rights.

In the case of *Venables v Newsgroup Newspapers [2001] The Times 16/1/01,* the court acknowledged the law of breach of confidence as a living and organic instrument, but applied the unseen and unacknowledged law of privacy. Although it is true that C was an alcoholic 22 years ago, it is likely that he will be harmed by this publication

In the case of *R v Broadcasting Complaints Commission, ex parte Granada Television Ltd TLR 16/12/94,* it was held that the showing of old footage from a previous programme in a broadcast without warning the persons concerned and their families was an unwarranted infringement of privacy.

The Court should take the stance similar to courts in France, Germany, Denmark, The Netherlands and Canada and treat this incursion of privacy as an offence requiring an injunction.

Argument 3.4: Article 10(2) ECHR is invoked.

Article 10 ECHR gives rise to 'the protection of the reputation or rights of others, for preventing the disclosure of information received in confidence' as well as the right to receive and impart information and ideas.

As Lord Phillips of Worth Matravers MR stated in *Ashdown v Sunday Telegraph Group Ltd [2001] EWCA Civ 1142* at paragraph 25, '.. there are many circumstances where freedom of expression must, of necessity be restricted.....Article 8 is an example.' More pertinent in this context is the right recognised by Article 1 of the first Protocol, which states '...no-one shall be deprived of his possessions except in the public interest and subject to the conditions provided by law and by the conditions of international law'.

C's copyright is clearly a possession to which attach all the rights associated with property, including peaceful enjoyment. It is a right arising from statute with which the court should not readily interfere. by refusing to issue an injunction against DMCI.

It is necessary and justified in a democratic society to restrict freedom of expression in order to protect copyright. It is submitted that it stretches the concept of freedom of expression too far to suggest that it extends to allow the freedom to convey the information in the form of words devised by C or anyone else. The ECHR expressly provides that the right to freedom of expression is nor absolute and a careful balancing act is required.

Argument 3.5: An immediate injunction should be granted.

The principles governing the granting of this interim injunction applied for were laid down by the House of Lords in *American Cyanamid v Ethicon [1975] AC 396*.

The American Cyanamid case was reviewed in the case of *Series 5 Software v Philip Clark & others [1996] FSR 273*.

IN the later case of *Microsoft Corp v Plato Technology [1999] FSR 834*, the key factor influencing the exercise of the court's decision was the defendant's state of mind. The defendant here, DMCI, has not acted innocently and had intended to infringe C" copyright. It is submitted that court must grant this injunction for the purpose of preventing future harm to C and to prevent repetition of copyright infringement.

Chronology

1980	Marco Polo diagnosed with incipient alcoholism.
1981	Marco Polo joined Addicts United to assist his recovery.
1982	Marco Polo writes article for 'For You Only'.
1983	'For You Only's secretary unofficially sent article to local public library.
1984	Devil-May-Care Ltd place article written by Marco Polo on website.

2003 IP MOOT (example 1—respondent's case)

<u>IN THE SUPREME COURT</u>   **Case No. 2003 POLO 0001**

BETWEEN

MARCO POLO
        <u>Claimant</u>

    and

DEVIL—MAY—CARE INTERNET COMPANY LIMITED   <u>Defendant</u>

1985   Introduction

1986   Background

1987   Argument

The Respondent's argument is based on the following submissions:

6.1   There was no infringement of copyright.

6.2   There was no breach of confidence.

6.3   There was no "right of privacy".

6.4   Article 10 European Convention On Human Rights apply and protects the web-site's activities.

6.5   The Appeal should be dismissed.

Argument 3.1: There was no infringement of copyright.

The reasons for this are that the publishing of the article on the web-site is argued to be in the public interest (*Kennard v Lewis [1983]*).

Also, it is argued that the article did not enjoy protection before 1988 and so the 1988 Copyright Design and Patents Act will not assist.

The article is already in a public library and so in the public domain.

It is not being used for commercial purposes.

It is also vehemently stated that the article being put on the web-site amounts to fair dealing. In *Newspaper Licensing Agency Ltd v Marks and Spencers plc (2001)*, Lightman. J held that "fair dealing" was concerned with the genuine cases of the *intentions and motives* of the use of the copyright material to report current events and the extent to which......it is fair and reasonable in all circumstances to make as extensive a use as was in fact made". Lightman. J. established a three stage test for raising a defence:

i) reporting current events; current events can include matters from the past and the copying of old sources because historical events can clearly be seen, as in this case, to be a source of 'contemporary news' (*Associated Newspapers plc v Newsgroup Newspapers Ltd [1986]*).

ii) fair dealing with the copyright work that is not an actual exploitation and

iii) acknowledgement. (*Stillitoe v McGraw-Hill Books [1983]*. There is no dispute as to the writer of the article.

Argument 3.2: There has been no breach of confidence.

The case of *Lord Advocate v The Scotsman Publications Ltd (1990)* supports this argument. In this case a former member of M16 published privately a book of memoirs dealing with the years 1948 to 1953. A total of 279 copies were distributed. The Lord Advocate sought an injunction restraining any publication of extracts of the book in "The Scotsman" newspaper. The case went to the House of Lords who refused to grant the injunction in the light of the fact that the book had already received some circulation (even though it was a very small number—279).

In support of this argument is another case *Lennon v News Group Newspaper Ltd (1978)*, in which the News Of The World Newspaper disclosed intimate details of the relationship between the former wife of John Lennon of the famous Beatles pop-group. John Lennon was denied an injunction because they were public personalities.

The key point in a breach of confidence issue is that one party tells something to another but expressly tells them that this is to be kept confidential. In this case the Claimant did not make an agreement with the AU publisher that they keep this article confidential.

Argument 3.3: There is no right of privacy in Erewhon Law.

In Erewhon, there is no privacy law because Erewhon's current law adequately protects privacy. If there were intrusion on the Claimant's property, he would have remedies against trespassing, harassing, photographing, watching using electronic devices, for example. If there were intrusion on the Claimant's body, the remedies would be assault and battery, wounding, for example. But the Claimant is a Member of Parliament and as such, automatically is watched and protected by the State system such as the Police and the Security services. The Claimant chose a profession which actively courts publicity.

Argument 3.4: Article 10 European Convention of Human Rights prevails.

This is a public interest matter and must be allowed to be revealed.

Argument 3.5: The appeal must be dismissed

To support the case that copyright was infringed

Copyright subsists in the article under the Copyright Act 1956. Since the article was written in 1980 the author, Polo, has copyright until the year 2030 unless he had signed an agreement to relinquish all his rights to AU.

It is implied that the AU publisher was only entitled to publish Polo's article in one particular publication.

Although there is a six year limitation for bringing a copyright claim and this has expired, Polo enjoys the exclusive rights of an author with regard to his original work and he has NOT granted a licence to the website provider.

The case of _Telstra (1997)_[7] raised the issue of liability for transmission of information on the Internet. The WIPO Copyright Treaty seeks to deal with the general questions of copyright infringement and liability in the digital era. It seems that although the Berne Convention does not cover the transmission of copyright material via the Internet unless transmission of that material has previously taken place by wireless means[8], Polo did not give authorisation to the website provider, nor did AU give permission for this transmission, the

---

7   Telstra Corp Ltd v Australasian Performing Right Association Ltd (1997) 146 ALR 649.

8   See article by Macmillan & Blakeney.

case of *NSW v Moorhouse*[9] shows that liability on copyright infringement can be imposed on the Internet provider irrespective of its ability to control the content of the transmissions and for authorising this infringement. (The lending of the article by the Public Library was the first breach[10]..)

The case to support Breach of Confidence

In *Naomi Campbell v MGN*[11], the judge held that in order to establish a claim for breach of confidence, three matters had to be established:

that the details published had "the necessary quality of confidence" about them;

that the details were imparted in circumstances importing an obligation of confidence and

that the publication of the details was to the plaintiff's detriment.

The first test was the requirement that disclosure or observation of information would be highly offensive to a reasonable person of ordinary sensibilities as in the case *Australian Broadcasting Corp v Lench Game Meats*[12]. It can be argued that the information that Polo was an alcoholic 22 years ago is highly offensive in light of the fact that he is in politics. It can be argued that information relating to Polo's former alcoholism, without details added that this is NOT the case now, satisfies this test.

The second test applied was that suggested by Lord Woolf in *A v B*[13] where he suggested that "usually the answer to the question whether there exists a private interest worthy of protection will be obvious". It can be argued that there exists a private interest worthy of protection in that Polo's career has progressed considerably since his student days 22 years ago and that the information about blip of alcoholism of 22 years ago would be disastrous to his career today. It can be argued that the article of 22 years ago bore the badge of confidentiality; it was written to encourage others to avoid alcohol and was written to provide therapeutic help to others in a special group of persons. If this had

---

9   NSW v Moorhouse (1975) 133 C.L.R. 1.

10   The Public Lending Right Act 1979 (UK).

11   Campbell v MGN Ltd (2002) EWCA 1373.

12   (2001) HCA 63 at paragraph 42.

13   A v B (2002) EWCA Civ 337; (2002) 3 WLR 542 at paragraph 11(vii)

been a newspaper article stating just that Polo, a student, was alcoholic, then it would have been in the public domain.

As to the third matter to be established, it can be argued that the publication of Polo's past brief alcoholism is clearly to his detriment and causes Polo considerable distress.

The case to support the Right of Privacy and NOT to the Right of Freedom of Expression

Devil-May-Care Internet Co. Ltd. were NOT entitled to publish the 22 year old article in the public interest under Article 10 Human Rights Act 1998 because this is qualified by Article 10(2). It can be argued that Article 8 Human Rights Act 1998, Right of Privacy, also qualifies the right to Freedom of Expression of Article 10. As in *Campbell v MGN*, there is no over-riding public interest duty to publish this 22 year old article. Article 8, Right to Privacy, should hold as Polo legitimately chose to keep this matter private today. It can be argued that Polo has NOT been misleading the public; he has NOT stated anywhere today that he NEVER had alcohol problems. Therefore this can be deemed a wrongful publication in breach of confidence details of a past private life. It can be argued that this is an infringement of privacy and a free-standing tort that has occurred because there is an intrusion into privacy. It is not topical.[14].

In Germany and France, it is an actionable wrong to publish without consent.

The Supreme Court should recognise this right of privacy and that Polo should have been approached before the article was put on the Internet. The information that Polo was briefly an alcoholic many years ago is a matter that Polo is entitled to keep confidential. Polo has never made any public pronouncements that he never did ever abuse alcohol.[15] Because Polo has achieved prominence on the public stage does not mean that his past private life can be laid bare by an Internet company. The publication of the article on the Internet was unjustified. Polo felt considerable distress at the revelation that he had long ago had a brief problem with alcohol. It is to be noted that in America there is a tort of breach of privacy. The relevant provisions in the Canadian and Quebec Charter are:

---

14   See case Cambridge Nutrition v BBC (1990) 3 All ER 523.

15   See A v B, paragraph 11 (xii) at paragraph 48. "Where an individual is a public figure, he is entitled to have his privacy respected in the appropriate circumstances. A public figure is entitled to a private life…".

Provision 4—"Every person has a right to safeguard his dignity, honour and reputation".

Provision 5—"Every person has a right to respect for his private life".

This right as per Provision 5 of the Quebec Charter is the same right as in the case of *Michael Douglas and others v Hello!*[16]. Furthermore, the right to respect for private and family life which is created by Article 8(9) of the European Convention on Human Rights, is similar to the Provision 5 of the Quebec Charter. Both owe their origin to Article 12 of the Universal Declaration of Human Rights, which states that:

"No-one shall be subjugated to arbitrary interference with his privacy, family, home and correspondence, nor to attacks on his honour and reputation. Everyone has the right to the protection of the law against such interference or attacks."[17] Besides, Polo has retained a right of veto over the publication of the article he wrote and so the element of privacy remains his.

Also, the case that the Internet company has the right to Freedom of Expression is false because the Internet company cannot be classed as Press and therefore cannot have freedom of expression as per the Press Complaints Commission Code of Practice for the UK.

This Press Code of Practice states:

"Privacy

Intrusion and inquiries into an individual's private life without his consent......are not generally acceptable and publication can only be justified when in the public interest".

The public's interest

Clauses 4,5,7,8 and 9 create exception which may be covered by evoking the public interest. For the purpose of this code that is most easily defined as:

Detecting or exposing crime or a serious misdemeanour.

Protecting public health or safety,

---

16 (2001) 2 All ER 289

17 See the case of Airey v Ireland 2 EHRR 305 and the case of X and Y v The Netherlands 8 EHRR 235.

Preventing the public being misled by some statement or action of an individual or organisation."

It can be strongly argued that the public interest was not served and so freedom of expression cannot be invoked.

Conclusion

The Appellant Polo has suffered loss in that his reputation has been damaged, his privacy has been invaded and he has suffered immense distress which is extremely difficult to quantify. The case of no infringement of copyright is incorrect. Copyright has been infringed.

2003 IP MOOT (example 2—appellant's case)

Polo v Devil-May-Care Internet Co. Ltd.

Submissions on Behalf of the Appellant

1   Introduction

This is an appeal by Marco Polo ("the appellant") against the decision of the High Court (affirmed by the Court of Appeal) in the above matter. The High Court refused to grant an injunction restraining the respondent from publishing on its website an article written by the appellant in 1980. This article was written for a newsletter entitled 'For You Only' for the benefit of 'Addicts United' ("AU") support group members. Without the consent of either the appellant or the group executive, copies of this newsletter were placed in a public library, where they were found by the respondent. The appellant alleges that the respondent's publication infringes the appellant's copyright, is in breach of confidence and infringes the appellant's human rights.

2   Copyright

2.1 Appellant Enjoys Copyright in the Article

As an "expression of thought"[18] by the appellant based on his own individual experiences, the article should enjoy copyright protection as an original literary work. It is recognised that ownership of copyright vests in the author, unless the work is created in the course of employment.[19] Accordingly AU could only have acquired ownership of copyright by virtue of an assignment. There is a consensus that such an assignment is ineffective unless in writing and signed by the assignor.[20] It follows that in the absence of any written assignment, the appellant remains the owner of copyright in the article. And that copyright must still subsist today. The standard term is reflected in the Berne Convention which allows for protection for the life of the author plus

---

18   University of London Press v University Tutorial Press [1916] 2 Ch. 601 at 608 per Peterson J

19   Sec. 11 UK Act 1988; sec. 23 Irish Act 2000. The appellant was not an employee of AU.

20   Sec. 120(3) Irish Act 2000; sec. 90(3) UK Act 1988.

fifty years.[21] This demonstrates that it is international practice to protect copyright at least until the end of the author's life.[22]

2.2 Nature of Exclusivity Conferred

Under the Berne Convention "*authors of literary…works…shall have the exclusive right of authorising the reproduction of these works, in any manner or form*".[23] Thus, the use by the respondent of the appellant's work without his permission, was an infringement of copyright. It was subsequently confirmed in the WIPO Copyright Treaty of 1996 that the author's exclusive rights extend to publication on the Internet.[24]

2.3 Exhaustion Doctrine Inapplicable

The owner's distribution right may be 'exhausted' with regard to a particular copy of his work after that copy has been made available with his consent.[25] The exhaustion doctrine entails an extinguishment of control on the part of the copyright owner over subsequent transfers in ownership of a copy of his work. It follows that there was no infringement of copyright when the AU secretary placed a copy of the newsletter in the public library. It is however

---

21 Article 7 of the Berne Convention for the Protection of Literary and Artistic Works. In the EU it is life of the author plus seventy years: Article 1(1) of Council Directive 93/98/EEC of 29 October 1993 harmonizing the term of protection of copyright and certain related rights [1993] OJ L 290/9.

22 After all, an author's efforts may not immediately be recognised or achieve significant returns. The principle goes to the heart of economic rights, which should not be limited, before they have even been properly exploited.

23 Article 9(1) Berne.

24 Article 8 provides as follows: "…authors of literary and artistic works shall enjoy the exclusive right of authorising any communication to the public of their works by wire or wireless means, including the making available to the public of their works in such a way that members of the public may access these works from a place and at a time individually chosen by them".

25 See Article 6 of the WIPO Copyright Treaty of 1996.

well-established that the exhaustion doctrine does not affect the right of the copyright owner to object to any subsequent reproduction of the work.[26]

2.4 No Implied Licence for the Respondent's Use

Where there is no express contract between author and publisher, the publisher has an implied licence to do what the author would reasonably expect the publisher to do. In *Ray v Classic FM*[27] the plaintiff was commissioned to create a work for the defendant and the defendant subsequently licensed other radio stations to use it. The court found that this was infringement of copyright and said that in determining the extent of an implied licence, the guide should be one of necessity: what kind of licence was necessary for the recipient to carry through its intended purpose? Accordingly where it was envisaged that AU would publish an article in a single issue of a newsletter, there would be no implied licence in respect of subsequent publications, and online publications[28]. Thus the further publication of the appellant's work would require his express permission even if such further publication was executed by AU. However, the respondent's website publication was not licensed by AU. The mere publication of a work by a licensee cannot create an entitlement on the part of others to republish the work.

2.5 Infringement of Appellant's Moral Rights

The Berne Convention provides that "the author shall have the right…to object to any distortion, mutilation or other modification of, or other derogatory action in relation to, [his] work, which would be prejudicial to his honour or reputation."[29] There has been a breach of the appellant's moral right to

---

26 This was accepted by the ECJ in Case 402/85 *Basset v SACEM* [1987] ECR 1747 and in Case 395/87 Ministière Public v Tournier [1989] ECR 2521. It follows also as a matter of principle that the exhaustion doctrine cannot affect the reproduction rights: otherwise the copyright owner would lose his exclusive rights on the first voluntary transfer of a copy and copyright would be worthless.

27 [1998] FSR 622.

28 The name of the article itself indicates that any implied licence was restricted to publication for the benefit of AU members.

29 Article 6bis.

object to derogatory action in relation to his work[30]. In *Beckett*[31] the French court held that the focus should be on the subjective reaction of the author. Here, the appellant's work has been stripped of its intended meaning through its use on the respondent's website.

3   Confidence

3.1 Article was not in the Public Domain

The High Court failed to recognise that the law of confidence is built around a notion of "*relative* secrecy". Courts have acknowledged that it is perfectly possible for a number of people to know about the "secret" and yet for the information to be regarded as being outside of the public domain.

In *Prince Albert v Strange*[32], for example, it was held that while Prince Albert had revealed his etchings to some friends, this did not destroy the confidentiality of the information. The appellant is in an analogous position in that his submission to 'For You Only' constituted disclosure to a small, defined group and so it was not released into the public domain. In *Douglas v Hello! Ltd*[33] a large number of people were privy to the confidence in question (the guests and staff at a wedding reception) but could not be equated with the "public domain". In *G v Day*[34], a revelation on TV did not strip the information in question of its confidentiality. In *Stephens v Avery*[35], Browne-Wilkinson V.-C. held that confidential information could remain such even where a group of people knew the facts, saying "*information only ceases to be capable of protection as confidential when it is in fact known to a substantial number of people*". Accordingly, factual rather than potential access to the information is the key factor. The geographical extent of the disclosure is also important. For example, in *Attorney General v Turnaround*[36] information which was widely available in Ireland was held to retain its confidential nature in the United Kingdom.

---

30   The UK has integrated this right into their law in the 1988 Copyright Act (sec. 80).
31   RIDA 1993, No. 155, 225. See also the Canadian case of Snow v Eaton Centre (1982) 70 CPR (2d) 105.
32   (1849) 2 DeG & Sm 652; 64 ER 293; (1849) 1 Mac & G 25, 41 ER 1171.
33   [2001] FSR 732.
34   [1982] 1 NSWLR 24
35   [1988] Ch. 449 at p 454.
36   [1989] FSR 169.

In determining the extent to which the article is in the public domain, the Court should not consider publicity arising from the respondent's own activities. To do so would be to allow the respondent to profit from his own wrongdoing.

Availability in one local library is not of sufficient magnitude to constitute release into the public domain. While a small number of people may have come across the article in the library, the appellant's recent popular support indicates that the confidential information has not yet reached the general public. This is not a case where there is no confidence left to protect. With the article now on the respondent's Internet site, however, there is a grave risk that a significant number of people may easily access the article to the detriment of the appellant. Bentley and Sherman[37] identify the extent to which *further* publication would harm the claimant as a major factor in indicating whether information remains confidential.

3.2 Duty of Confidence Arises in the Absence of a Direct Relationship

It has long been recognised that third parties who receive information innocently, but subsequently discover the confidential nature of the information, are bound by a duty of confidence[38]. The respondent knew, or ought to have known, that the information in the article was confidential[39]. The test is no longer whether the "stranger" is acting illegally, but whether anything reasonably leads the observer to realise that what he or she observes is confidential[40]. This is a necessary and sensible approach since otherwise the right of action in confidence could always be thwarted by the passing on of the information by the direct recipient.

---

37 Bently & Sherman Intellectual Property Law (OUP, 2001) at p 929.

38 Stephenson Jordan & Harrison v MacDonald & Evans (1951) 68 RPC 190; (1952) 69 RPC 10; Hoechst v Chemiculture [1993] FSR 270; Cadbury Schweppes v FBI Foods [2000] FSR 491 at p 504 (Supr. Ct. of Canada). See Bently & Sherman (supra) at p 944.

39 In AG v Guardian Newspapers (No. 2) [1990] AC 109 at p 260 ('the Spycatcher case'), Lord Keith said "[i]t is a general rule of law that a third party who comes into possession of confidential information which he knows to be such, may come under a duty not to pass it on to anyone else."

40 AG v Guardian Newspapers [1990] AC 109.

The respondent, on seeing a newsletter entitled "For You Only", a volume obviously circulated to the type of support group which invariably protects its members' anonymity, must have realised that a mistake had been made for the newsletter to appear in a public library. Knowledge has been held to include circumstances where the disclosee has deliberately closed his eyes to the obvious.[41] Even if the court is satisfied that the respondent was unaware of the confidential nature of the information, it should not be allowed to continue to publish the information now that it has been fixed with knowledge of its confidentiality.

3.3 No Public Interest Defence

It can hardly be argued that it is in the public interest to disclose details of a personal alcohol problem conquered 23 years ago. The "public interest defence" is confined to misdeeds of a serious nature and importance to the country[42]. The recent case of *Campbell v MGN*[43] is distinguishable in that the plaintiff in that case had committed a criminal offence in taking narcotic substances, and had previously gone out of her way to aver that she did not take drugs. Further, she had conceded that the media were entitled to set the record straight on her drugs problem, and the authority of *Campbell* is severely confined by this concession. Alcohol is not a prohibited substance. The appellant did not mislead the public as the plaintiff in *Campbell* did.

The respondent's motives are relevant here. It published the confidential information with a view to increasing interest in its website and thereby securing greater future advertising revenue.[44] The respondent here is confusing its own interest with that of the public[45].

The Court should be concerned to confine the public interest defence. There can be no general exception in respect of making the truth known because the action is concerned with protecting against the disclosure of *true* information.

---

41 AG v Guardian Newspapers [1990] AC 109, 281-2; Thomas v Pearce [2000] FSR 718.

42 Beloff v Pressdram [1973] 1 All ER 241 at p 260.

43 Unreported (English Ct of Appeal, 14th October 2002).

44 It is commonplace for Internet-based enterprises nowadays to receive remuneration from companies advertising on their websites.

45 Lord Denning MR observed in Initial Services v Putterill [1968] 1 QB 396 at p 406 that "[i]t is a great evil when people purvey scandalous information for reward".

Where the exception is too widely drawn as in *Woodward v Hutchins*,[46] the result is uncertainty and a proliferation of litigation and the defence becomes "not so much a rule of law as an invitation to judicial idiosyncrasy".[47]

4 Invasion of the Appellant's Human Rights

The European Convention[48] imposes positive obligations[49] on States to protect the right to privacy.[50] The margin of appreciation enjoyed by States in fulfilling this obligation must provide a fair balance between the competing interests of the individual and of the community.[51] The right to freedom of expression only embraces issues of current public interest. The appellant's alcohol addiction is not of public interest as he has not suffered from the addiction for over 22 years.[52]

---

46 [1977] 2 All ER 751.

47 Smith Kline & French v Department of Community Health [1990] FSR 617 at p 663, per Gummow J.. Cited by Bently & Sherman at p 966. Gummow J. asserted that equitable principles are best developed by reference to what conscionable behaviour demands of the defendant (see Bently & Sherman at p 966). In this instance, it is unconscionable to capitalise (especially for remuneration) on a breach of confidence that stands to damage the reputation of a hard-working political reformist.

48 Convention for the Protection of Human Rights and Fundamental Freedoms.

49 X and Y v The Netherlands EHRR. 235 (1985), also Airey v Ireland 2 EHRR. 305 (1979). Although Convention rights are not held to be actionable against private individuals, indirect horizontal effect can be said to apply through the obligation of courts. The courts of signatories to the Convention are public authorities themselves and so are in principle bound to apply the law in line with Convention rights. See Phillipson & Fenwick "Breach of Confidence as a Privacy Remedy in the Human Rights Act Era" (2000) 63 MLR 660 at p 667.

50 Set down in Article 8.

51 Lopez-Ostra v Spain 9th December 1994, Series A, No. 303-C, 20 EHRR 277, para 51. This fair balance should be established using the test of proportionality: Douglas v Hello! Ltd. [2001] FSR 732.

52 Issues of public interest must be at issue at the time they are being put in the public arena: *Associated Newspapers v News Group* [1986] RPC 515; here, the death of the Duchess of Windsor did not justify the publication of an exchange of letters between the Duchess and the Duke.

It was acknowledged in a recent U.K. case that political speech (defined as "discussion of public affairs generally"[53]) enjoys a wider margin of appreciation in the extent to which it can include detail of private life. However, the appellant's article was concerned with a private rather than a public affair.

Winer v UK[54] demonstrates how the court generally gives a wide margin to the legislating state. This case, however, left open the possibility of imposing an obligation to provide a remedy, where an invasion related exclusively to truthful information.[55] In *Earl Spencer v UK*[56] the court found that confidence as a domestic remedy had not been exhausted. Notably, however, the Court did not find that there had been no breach of Article 8. Both cases support the proposition that where existing domestic remedies fail to meet the protection of Article 8 rights, national courts must create a new remedy.

Finally, the right to privacy should not be ranked lower than freedom of expression. In the U.S., this 'hierarchy' has led to an extinction of privacy rights.[57] Balancing both rights properly, the respondent's invasion of the appellant's privacy was disproportionate and unrelated to any legitimate aim in a democratic society.

5   Interlocutory Application

Finally, in applying the American Cyanamid[58] test, there is a serious issue to be tried for the reasons set out above. Given the potential for destruction of the appellant's reputation and the inevitable difficulty of assessing damages should the appellant succeed at trial, the balance of convenience favours granting the injunction.

---

53   Reynolds v Times Newspaper [1999] 4 All ER 609.

54   48 IR 154 (1986).

55   In this case, however, the court found that the provision of a defamation remedy for the untruthful statements at issue was sufficient to protect privacy.

56   25 EHRR. CD 105 (1998).

57   Due to the absolute nature of the First Amendment. The Convention has been interpreted in Germany, France, Canada and Britain as giving rise to an equal balancing of both rights in individual situations. In a German case, the Supreme Court remarked that "neither can claim precedence in principle over the other": Bverf GE 35 200. See Phillipson & Fenwick (supra) at p 686.

58   [1975] AC 396

EXAMPLE TWO—RESPONDENT'S CASE—IP MOOT 2003

Polo (Appellant) v

Devil-May-Care Internet Co. Ltd. (Respondent)

1   Introduction

The respondent has published on its website an article written by the appellant and describing his experience of alcoholism. The High Court of Erewhon decided that the respondent did not infringe copyright or breach any right in confidence or any human right in so doing. This decision was affirmed by the Court of Appeal. The respondent asks this Court to dismiss the appellant's further appeal on the following grounds.

2   Human Rights

2.1   Freedom of Expression: General

"Freedom of Expression constitutes one of the essential foundations of a [democratic] society, of the basic conditions for its progress and for the development of every man...it is applicable not only to "information" or "ideas" that are favourably received or regarded as inoffensive, but also to those that offend, shock or disturb the state or any sector of the population. Such are the demands of that pluralism, tolerance and broadmindedness without which there is no democratic society"[59]

The European Court of Human Rights (ECHR) in *Handyside* gave two reasons for the importance of this right:

(i) Central importance to the functioning of a democratic society: political representatives can only understand and represent the views of their constituents through an open, two-way process of airing views, opinions and *facts*.

(ii) Persons can only achieve self-fulfilment and their full human potential through being able to freely communicate their feelings, opinions and ideas.[60]

---

59   Handyside v UK, Series A, No. 24; 1 EHRR 737 (1979-80).

60   Janis, Kay and Bradley, European Human Rights Law, (Clarendon, 1995), p 157.

The respondent submits that this important right would be infringed if an injunction were to be granted suppressing the publication of the appellant's article. It is of the utmost importance that the public know of his history of alcoholism if they are to make a fully informed decision as to whether or not he should be elected as their representative.

2.2 Freedom of Expression and the Politician

In *Lingens v Austria*[61] the ECHR imported a concept from the US Supreme Court that politicians must expect and tolerate greater public scrutiny and criticism than other citizens. It stressed the media's crucial role in reporting matters of public interest. Freedom of the press provided the public with "one of the best means of discovering and forming an opinion of the ideas and attitudes of political leaders"[62]. The court also stated that "[t]he limits of acceptable criticism are accordingly wider as regards a politician as such than as regards a private individual"[63]. In *Sunday Times v UK*[64] the ECHR said that the Freedom of Expression (Article 10) guarantee, not only includes "the freedom of the press to inform the public, but also the right of the public to be properly informed."[65] A person who is a recovering alcoholic and is standing for election, is placing himself in the public eye and presenting himself as a responsible and suitable person for public office. The public has a right to put him under thorough scrutiny as to his suitability for office.

2.3 Freedom of Expression and the Margin of Appreciation

The court's restriction of the margin of appreciation in relation to Article 10 was demonstrated in the *Spycatcher case*[66]. A distinction was drawn between two time periods before and after the controversial book was published in the US. In relation to the first time period it ruled that the injunctions against the publication were justified because of a risk that the material was prejudicial to the British Secret Service. In relation to the second period, the court ruled unanimously that Article 10 had been violated. The government's aim of protecting

---

61   Series A, No. 103; 8 EHHR 103 (1986).

62   Ibid at p 419.

63   Ibid.

64   Sunday Times v UK, Series A, No. 30; 2 EHHR 245.

65   Ibid p 277-282.

66   Observer and Guardian v UK, Series A, No 216; 14 EHHR 153.

confidentiality was no longer relevant as the information had entered the public domain. The court reiterated that freedom of expression is not to be balanced against other interests but is "subject to a number of exceptions which…must be narrowly interpreted"[67] The appellant's right to privacy was not breached as the article was no longer private. It had already been made available in the public library. The interests of the appellant in restricting the publication are not sufficient to meet the narrow limits of a permissible exception to the Article 10 right.

2.4 Freedom of Expression and Prior Censorship

The American Convention on Human Rights preserves a wide concept of freedom of expression protecting, not only the right to express thoughts but to receive information, to ensure the function of democracy and the free exchange of ideas in the public forum. The right "shall not be subject to prior censorship"[68]. This ensures that no preventative measures are used but only subsequent imposition of sanctions on those who are guilty of abuses.[69] An injunction against the respondent should not be granted, since the appellant has not made out a sufficient case at this interlocutory stage[70].

3 Copyright

3.1 Copyright as an Instrument of Censorship

Addressing the House of Commons in 1841 Macauley remarked as follows: "It is desirable that we should have a supply of good books: we cannot have such a supply unless men of letters are liberally remunerated: and the least objectionable way of remunerating them is by means of copyright."[71] Writing in the Columbia Law Review in 1945, Chafee described copyright as facilitating "the

---

67 Ibid.

68 Art 13(2) American Convention of Human Rights. Laddie J. one of the UK's leading intellectual property judges, has indicated the UK should consider adopting a more general defence.

69 Appeal to the Inter American Commission on Human Rights in the "Diplomatic Impunity" case, Report No. 11/96, case 11.230-Chile, May 3 1996

70 This presents a precedent for reducing the restriction of the Right to Freedom of Expression to the extent that no interlocutory procedures can be justified where this right is concerned.

71 Cited by Chafee "Reflections on the Law of Copyright I" (1945) 4 Columbia Law Review, 503 at p 507.

free flow of ideas and imaginative ideas across national boundaries".[72] Copyright was thus conceived as a means of promoting education and the exchange of information and ideas. Copyright was not intended to provide a vehicle for censorship and the suppression of information and this Court should not permit its abuse for that purpose.

3.2 Enforcement of Copyright Contrary to Public Policy/Interest

In *Glyn v Weston Feature Film Co.*[73] Younger J. held that copyright could not subsist in a "grossly immoral work". The House of Lords in *AG v Guardian Newspapers ("Spycatcher")*[74] indicated that the courts would not enforce a claim to copyright in a work where its publication was contrary to the public interest. This reflects a broader principle that copyright protection should be denied to those who seek to exercise it in a manner which clearly offends the public interest. In *Ashdown v Telegraph Group*[75] the Court of Appeal confirmed that the public interest could justify the publication of work against the wishes of the copyright-owner even in the absence of wrongdoing on his part. There is a strong public interest in revealing that the appellant who is so strongly opposed to alcohol consumption, was himself diagnosed as suffering from incipient alcoholism.

3.3 Fair Dealing

In *Ashdown v Telegraph Group* the Court of Appeal accepted that the most important factor relevant to the defence of fair dealing is whether the alleged infringer is commercially competing with the proprietor's exploitation of the copyright work. The court supported the view expressed in *Laddie, Prescott & Vitoria*[76] that where there is no competition the defence is likely to succeed "if the defendant's additional purpose is to right a wrong, to ventilate an honest grievance, to engage in political controversy...". The court accepted that the second most important factor is whether the work has already been published or otherwise exposed to the public and said that the defence is likely to fail where unpublished information has been obtained by some

---

72 Ibid. at p 506.
73 [1916] 1 Ch. 261 at p 269.
74 [1990] 1 AC 109 at p 262, per Lord Keith.
75 [2002] Ch. 149 at p 173.
76 The Modern Law of Copyright and Designs (3rd Ed., 2000).

underhand dealing. And finally the court identified the extent of the taking as being the third most important factor.

Whilst the respondent did publish the whole of the appellant's article, it was not competing with the appellant in any way and it did not deprive the appellant of any commercial benefit which he might otherwise have derived from that work. Moreover, the respondent was publishing a work which had previously been published with the consent of the appellant and which it obtained in a public library.

3.4 Copyright Interfering with Confidence

The law of confidence is concerned with striking an appropriate balance between free speech and privacy. This Court should not allow copyright to upset the careful balance established by the law of confidence.

4 Confidence

4.1 Information already in public domain and thus incapable of being protected

The status of information is a question of fact, not intention. If material is in fact in the public domain, it is irrelevant that the confider intended that it be kept secret. It is clear from *Mustad v Allcock and Dosen*[77] that once the disclosee publishes the information, the obligation of confidence comes to an end. Here, the information was freely accessible to the general public in a State library. That this was not intended by the appellant is irrelevant.

The degree of publication is relevant, but the publication here was more than sufficient. Indeed, Bently and Sherman[78] note in this regard that "[a]s Internet use grows, it will be increasingly difficult for a claimant to establish that information known in one place is confidential elsewhere".

AG v Guardian Newspapers[79] ("Spycatcher") is powerful authority for the respondent's case. In this decision, the House of Lords held that once information was in

---

77 (1928) [1963] 3 All ER 416. Cited by Bently and Sherman Intellectual Property Law (2001, OUP).

78 Bently and Sherman at p 929.

79 [1987] 1 WLR 1248.

the public domain the courts could not restrain further publication, even if the information entered the public domain via a breach of confidence.

4.2 No Obligation on Respondent to Keep Information Confidential

Coco v Clark[80] requires that there exist on the part of the respondent an obligation to keep the information confidential. The parties in this case are not in any contractual or fiduciary relationship. The respondent was an indirect recipient of information and not party to any relationship of confidence. It is unreasonable to suggest that a person who came across information in a public library, freely available to the general public, was grossly negligent in failing to realise that a breach of confidence was involved, and this is the standard set down in *AG v Guardian Newspapers*. It is not sufficient to show that the failure to appreciate the confidential nature of the information was "merely careless, naïve or stupid" (*Thomas v Pearce*).[81]

4.3 Public Interest Defence

Wood V.-C. in *Gartside v Outram*[82] famously said: "there is no confidence as to the disclosure of iniquity". The case of *Initial Services v Putterill*[83] established that the concept of "iniquity" embraces not only crime or fraud, but any misconduct of such a nature that it is in the public interest to disclose it. This view was reasserted by Lord Denning in *Fraser v Evans*[84]. While it is generally accepted that a distinction must be drawn between information which is interesting to the public and information, the disclosure of which is in the public interest, this case is a clearly in the latter category. The appellant is seeking public office on a pledge of zero tolerance regarding drug and alcohol offences. Where a politician bases his campaign on a condemnation of certain practices, the public has an interest in knowing whether he has ever engaged in such practices himself. Such information is relevant to the public's assessment of the sincerity and the objectivity of the politician in adopting such an agenda.

---

80   [1968] FSR 415.
81   [2000] FSR 718. See also Shelley Films v Rex Features [1994] EMLR 134; (third party only on notice when must have seen signs specifically prohibiting taking of photographs); also Douglas v Hello [2001] FSR 732.
82   (1857) 26 LJ Ch 113
83   [1968] 1 QB 396
84   [1969] 1 All ER 8

Moreover, it is generally accepted by psychologists that alcoholics are never fully 'cured' of their affliction in the common sense of the word. Voters are entitled to be appraised of facts which may affect the ability of a politician to carry out his duties in public office.

Campbell v MGN[85] lends strong support to the respondent's claim. Here, it was held that the public interest defence operated to justify disclosure of the appellant's narcotic abuse. The appellant was a supermodel celebrity, with no professional responsibility to the public. *A fortiori*, the double standards and dishonesty of a potential public servant and MP deserve to be disclosed to the public so that they may make an informed choice in the parliamentary elections.

5   Interlocutory Injunctive Relief

The automatic grant of interim relief based on the test developed in *American Cyanamid v Ethicon*[86] would have grave implications for freedom of expression[87]. The dangers associated with such a policy have been recognised by the English legislature in the 1998 Human Rights Act which establishes that where the relief sought encroaches upon freedom of expression a claimant must show that there is more than a serious issue to be tried.

Polo v Devil-May-Care Internet Co. Ltd.

Submissions on Behalf of the Appellant

1   Introduction

This is an appeal by Marco Polo ("the appellant") against the decision of the High Court (affirmed by the Court of Appeal) in the above matter. The High Court refused to grant an injunction restraining the respondent from publishing on its website an article written by the appellant in 1980. This article was

---

85   [2002] EWCA Civ 1373

86   [1975] AC 396

87   See Hubbard v Vosper [1972]; Cambridge Nutrition v BBC [1990]; Times v Mirror Group [1993] where the application of American Cyanamid was eschewed in favour of a more detailed examination of the merits of the parties' claims.

written for a newsletter entitled 'For You Only' for the benefit of 'Addicts United' ("AU") support group members. Without the consent of either the appellant or the group executive, copies of this newsletter were placed in a public library, where they were found by the respondent. The appellant alleges that the respondent's publication infringes the appellant's copyright, is in breach of confidence and infringes the appellant's human rights.

2 Copyright

2.1 Appellant Enjoys Copyright in the Article

As an "expression of thought"[88] by the appellant based on his own individual experiences, the article should enjoy copyright protection as an original literary work. It is recognised that ownership of copyright vests in the author, unless the work is created in the course of employment.[89] Accordingly AU could only have acquired ownership of copyright by virtue of an assignment. There is a consensus that such an assignment is ineffective unless in writing and signed by the assignor.[90] It follows that in the absence of any written assignment, the appellant remains the owner of copyright in the article. And that copyright must still subsist today. The standard term is reflected in the Berne Convention which allows for protection for the life of the author plus fifty years.[91] This demonstrates that it is international practice to protect copyright at least until the end of the author's life.[92]

---

88 University of London Press v University Tutorial Press [1916] 2 Ch. 601 at 608 per Peterson J

89 Sec. 11 UK Act 1988; sec. 23 Irish Act 2000. The appellant was not an employee of AU.

90 Sec. 120(3) Irish Act 2000; sec. 90(3) UK Act 1988.

91 Article 7 of the Berne Convention for the Protection of Literary and Artistic Works. In the EU it is life of the author plus seventy years: Article 1(1) of Council Directive 93/98/EEC of 29 October 1993 harmonizing the term of protection of copyright and certain related rights [1993] OJ L 290/9.

92 After all, an author's efforts may not immediately be recognised or achieve significant returns. The principle goes to the heart of economic rights, which should not be limited, before they have even been properly exploited.

2.2 Nature of Exclusivity Conferred

Under the Berne Convention "*authors of literary…works…shall have the exclusive right of authorising the reproduction of these works, in any manner or form*".[93] Thus, the use by the respondent of the appellant's work without his permission, was an infringement of copyright. It was subsequently confirmed in the WIPO Copyright Treaty of 1996 that the author's exclusive rights extend to publication on the Internet.[94]

2.3 Exhaustion Doctrine Inapplicable

The owner's distribution right may be 'exhausted' with regard to a particular copy of his work after that copy has been made available with his consent.[95] The exhaustion doctrine entails an extinguishment of control on the part of the copyright owner over subsequent transfers in ownership of a copy of his work. It follows that there was no infringement of copyright when the AU secretary placed a copy of the newsletter in the public library. It is however well-established that the exhaustion doctrine does not affect the right of the copyright owner to object to any subsequent reproduction of the work.[96]

2.4 No Implied Licence for the Respondent's Use

Where there is no express contract between author and publisher, the publisher has an implied licence to do what the author would reasonably expect the publisher to do. In *Ray v Classic FM*[97] the plaintiff was commissioned to

---

93 Article 9(1) Berne.

94 Article 8 provides as follows: "…authors of literary and artistic works shall enjoy the exclusive right of authorising any communication to the public of their works by wire or wireless means, including the making available to the public of their works in such a way that members of the public may access these works from a place and at a time individually chosen by them".

95 See Article 6 of the WIPO Copyright Treaty of 1996.

96 This was accepted by the ECJ in Case 402/85 *Basset v SACEM* [1987] ECR 1747 and in Case 395/87 Ministière Public v Tournier [1989] ECR 2521. It follows also as a matter of principle that the exhaustion doctrine cannot affect the reproduction rights: otherwise the copyright owner would lose his exclusive rights on the first voluntary transfer of a copy and copyright would be worthless.

97 [1998] FSR 622.

create a work for the defendant and the defendant subsequently licensed other radio stations to use it. The court found that this was infringement of copyright and said that in determining the extent of an implied licence, the guide should be one of necessity: what kind of licence was necessary for the recipient to carry through its intended purpose? Accordingly where it was envisaged that AU would publish an article in a single issue of a newsletter, there would be no implied licence in respect of subsequent publications, and online publications[98]. Thus the further publication of the appellant's work would require his express permission even if such further publication was executed by AU. However, the respondent's website publication was not licensed by AU. The mere publication of a work by a licensee cannot create an entitlement on the part of others to republish the work.

2.5 Infringement of Appellant's Moral Rights

The Berne Convention provides that "the author shall have the right…to object to any distortion, mutilation or other modification of, or other derogatory action in relation to, [his] work, which would be prejudicial to his honour or reputation."[99] There has been a breach of the appellant's moral right to object to derogatory action in relation to his work[100]. In *Beckett*[101] the French court held that the focus should be on the subjective reaction of the author. Here, the appellant's work has been stripped of its intended meaning through its use on the respondent's website.

3   Confidence

3.1 Article was not in the Public Domain

The High Court failed to recognise that the law of confidence is built around a notion of "*relative* secrecy". Courts have acknowledged that it is perfectly possible for a number of people to know about the "secret" and yet for the information to be regarded as being outside of the public domain.

---

98 The name of the article itself indicates that any implied licence was restricted to publication for the benefit of AU members.

99 Article 6bis.

100 The UK has integrated this right into their law in the 1988 Copyright Act (sec. 80).

101 RIDA 1993, No. 155, 225. See also the Canadian case of Snow v Eaton Centre (1982) 70 CPR (2d) 105.

In *Prince Albert v Strange*[102], for example, it was held that while Prince Albert had revealed his etchings to some friends, this did not destroy the confidentiality of the information. The appellant is in an analogous position in that his submission to 'For You Only' constituted disclosure to a small, defined group and so it was not released into the public domain. In *Douglas v Hello! Ltd*[103] a large number of people were privy to the confidence in question (the guests and staff at a wedding reception) but could not be equated with the "public domain". In *G v Day*[104], a revelation on TV did not strip the information in question of its confidentiality. In *Stephens v Avery*[105], Browne-Wilkinson V.-C. held that confidential information could remain such even where a group of people knew the facts, saying *"information only ceases to be capable of protection as confidential when it is in fact known to a substantial number of people"*. Accordingly, factual rather than potential access to the information is the key factor. The geographical extent of the disclosure is also important. For example, in *Attorney General v Turnaround*[106] information which was widely available in Ireland was held to retain its confidential nature in the United Kingdom.

In determining the extent to which the article is in the public domain, the Court should not consider publicity arising from the respondent's own activities. To do so would be to allow the respondent to profit from his own wrongdoing.

Availability in one local library is not of sufficient magnitude to constitute release into the public domain. While a small number of people may have come across the article in the library, the appellant's recent popular support indicates that the confidential information has not yet reached the general public. This is not a case where there is no confidence left to protect. With the article now on the respondent's Internet site, however, there is a grave risk that a significant number of people may easily access the article to the detriment of the appellant. Bentley and Sherman[107] identify the extent to which *further* publication would harm the claimant as a major factor in indicating whether information remains confidential.

---

102 (1849) 2 DeG & Sm 652; 64 ER 293; (1849) 1 Mac & G 25, 41 ER 1171.
103 [2001] FSR 732.
104 [1982] 1 NSWLR 24
105 [1988] Ch. 449 at p 454.
106 [1989] FSR 169.
107 Bently & Sherman Intellectual Property Law (OUP, 2001) at p 929.

3.2 Duty of Confidence Arises in the Absence of a Direct Relationship

It has long been recognised that third parties who receive information innocently, but subsequently discover the confidential nature of the information,
are bound by a duty of confidence[108]. The respondent knew, or ought to have
known, that the information in the article was confidential[109]. The test is no
longer whether the "stranger" is acting illegally, but whether anything reasonably leads the observer to realise that what he or she observes is confidential[110]. This is a necessary and sensible approach since otherwise the right of
action in confidence could always be thwarted by the passing on of the information by the direct recipient.

The respondent, on seeing a newsletter entitled "For You Only", a volume obviously circulated to the type of support group which invariably protects its
members' anonymity, must have realised that a mistake had been made for the
newsletter to appear in a public library. Knowledge has been held to include
circumstances where the disclosee has deliberately closed his eyes to the obvious.[111] Even if the court is satisfied that the respondent was unaware of the
confidential nature of the information, it should not be allowed to continue to
publish the information now that it has been fixed with knowledge of its confidentiality.

3.3 No Public Interest Defence

It can hardly be argued that it is in the public interest to disclose details of a
personal alcohol problem conquered 23 years ago. The "public interest
defence" is confined to misdeeds of a serious nature and importance to the

---

108 Stephenson Jordan & Harrison v MacDonald & Evans (1951) 68 RPC 190; (1952)
     69 RPC 10; Hoechst v Chemiculture [1993] FSR 270; Cadbury Schweppes v FBI
     Foods [2000] FSR 491 at p 504 (Supr. Ct. of Canada). See Bently & Sherman
     (supra) at p 944.
109 In AG v Guardian Newspapers (No. 2) [1990] AC 109 at p 260 ('the Spycatcher
     case'), Lord Keith said "[i]t is a general rule of law that a third party who comes
     into possession of confidential information which he knows to be such, may come
     under a duty not to pass it on to anyone else."
110 AG v Guardian Newspapers [1990] AC 109.
111 AG v Guardian Newspapers [1990] AC 109, 281-2; Thomas v Pearce [2000] FSR
     718.

country[112]. The recent case of *Campbell v MGN*[113] is distinguishable in that the plaintiff in that case had committed a criminal offence in taking narcotic substances, and had previously gone out of her way to aver that she did not take drugs. Further, she had conceded that the media were entitled to set the record straight on her drugs problem, and the authority of *Campbell* is severely confined by this concession. Alcohol is not a prohibited substance. The appellant did not mislead the public as the plaintiff in *Campbell* did.

The respondent's motives are relevant here. It published the confidential information with a view to increasing interest in its website and thereby securing greater future advertising revenue.[114] The respondent here is confusing its own interest with that of the public[115].

The Court should be concerned to confine the public interest defence. There can be no general exception in respect of making the truth known because the action is concerned with protecting against the disclosure of *true* information. Where the exception is too widely drawn as in *Woodward v Hutchins*,[116] the result is uncertainty and a proliferation of litigation and the defence becomes "not so much a rule of law as an invitation to judicial idiosyncrasy".[117]

---

112 Beloff v Pressdram [1973] 1 All ER 241 at p 260.

113 Unreported (English Ct of Appeal, 14th October 2002).

114 It is commonplace for Internet-based enterprises nowadays to receive remuneration from companies advertising on their websites.

115 Lord Denning MR observed in Initial Services v Putterill [1968] 1 QB 396 at p 406 that "[i]t is a great evil when people purvey scandalous information for reward".

116 [1977] 2 All ER 751.

117 Smith Kline & French v Department of Community Health [1990] FSR 617 at p 663, per Gummow J,. Cited by Bently & Sherman at p 966. Gummow J. asserted that equitable principles are best developed by reference to what conscionable behaviour demands of the defendant (see Bently & Sherman at p 966). In this instance, it is unconscionable to capitalise (especially for remuneration) on a breach of confidence that stands to damage the reputation of a hard-working political reformist.

4 Invasion of the Appellant's Human Rights

The European Convention[118] imposes positive obligations[119] on States to protect the right to privacy.[120] The margin of appreciation enjoyed by States in fulfilling this obligation must provide a fair balance between the competing interests of the individual and of the community.[121] The right to freedom of expression only embraces issues of current public interest. The appellant's alcohol addiction is not of public interest as he has not suffered from the addiction for over 22 years.[122]

It was acknowledged in a recent U.K. case that political speech (defined as "discussion of public affairs generally"[123]) enjoys a wider margin of appreciation in the extent to which it can include detail of private life. However, the appellant's article was concerned with a private rather than a public affair.

Winer v UK[124] demonstrates how the court generally gives a wide margin to the legislating state. This case, however, left open the possibility of imposing an obligation to provide a remedy, where an invasion related exclusively to truthful information.[125] In *Earl Spencer v UK*[126] the court found that confidence as

---

118 Convention for the Protection of Human Rights and Fundamental Freedoms.

119 X and Y v The Netherlands EHRR. 235 (1985), also Airey v Ireland 2 EHRR. 305 (1979). Although Convention rights are not held to be actionable against private individuals, indirect horizontal effect can be said to apply through the obligation of courts. The courts of signatories to the Convention are public authorities themselves and so are in principle bound to apply the law in line with Convention rights. See Phillipson & Fenwick "Breach of Confidence as a Privacy Remedy in the Human Rights Act Era" (2000) 63 MLR 660 at p 667.

120 Set down in Article 8.

121 Lopez-Ostra v Spain 9th December 1994, Series A, No. 303-C, 20 EHRR 277, para 51. This fair balance should be established using the test of proportionality: Douglas v Hello! Ltd. [2001] FSR 732.

122 Issues of public interest must be at issue at the time they are being put in the public arena: *Associated Newspapers v News Group* [1986] RPC 515; here, the death of the Duchess of Windsor did not justify the publication of an exchange of letters between the Duchess and the Duke.

123 Reynolds v Times Newspaper [1999] 4 All ER 609.

124 48 IR 154 (1986).

125 In this case, however, the court found that the provision of a defamation remedy for the untruthful statements at issue was sufficient to protect privacy.

126 25 EHRR. CD 105 (1998).

a domestic remedy had not been exhausted. Notably, however, the Court did not find that there had been no breach of Article 8. Both cases support the proposition that where existing domestic remedies fail to meet the protection of Article 8 rights, national courts must create a new remedy.

Finally, the right to privacy should not be ranked lower than freedom of expression. In the U.S., this 'hierarchy' has led to an extinction of privacy rights.[127] Balancing both rights properly, the respondent's invasion of the appellant's privacy was disproportionate and unrelated to any legitimate aim in a democratic society.

5 Interlocutory Application

Finally, in applying the American Cyanamid[128] test, there is a serious issue to be tried for the reasons set out above. Given the potential for destruction of the appellant's reputation and the inevitable difficulty of assessing damages should the appellant succeed at trial, the balance of convenience favours granting the injunction.

---

127 Due to the absolute nature of the First Amendment. The Convention has been interpreted in Germany, France, Canada and Britain as giving rise to an equal balancing of both rights in individual situations. In a German case, the Supreme Court remarked that "neither can claim precedence in principle over the other": Bverf GE 35 200. See Phillipson & Fenwick (supra) at p 686.

128 [1975] AC 396

2003 IP MOOT (example 2—respondent's case)

Polo (Appellant) v

Devil-May-Care Internet Co. Ltd. (Respondent)

1   Introduction

The respondent has published on its website an article written by the appellant and describing his experience of alcoholism. The High Court of Erewhon decided that the respondent did not infringe copyright or breach any right in confidence or any human right in so doing. This decision was affirmed by the Court of Appeal. The respondent asks this Court to dismiss the appellant's further appeal on the following grounds.

2   Human Rights

2.1   Freedom of Expression: General

"Freedom of Expression constitutes one of the essential foundations of a [democratic] society, of the basic conditions for its progress and for the development of every man…it is applicable not only to "information" or "ideas" that are favourably received or regarded as inoffensive, but also to those that offend, shock or disturb the state or any sector of the population. Such are the demands of that pluralism, tolerance and broadmindedness without which there is no democratic society"[129]

The European Court of Human Rights (ECHR) in *Handyside* gave two reasons for the importance of this right:

Central importance to the functioning of a democratic society: political representatives can only understand and represent the views of their constituents through an open, two-way process of airing views, opinions and *facts*.

Persons can only achieve self-fulfilment and their full human potential through being able to freely communicate their feelings, opinions and ideas.[130]

---

129 Handyside v UK, Series A, No. 24; 1 EHRR 737 (1979-80).

130 Janis, Kay and Bradley, European Human Rights Law, (Clarendon, 1995), p 157.

The respondent submits that this important right would be infringed if an injunction were to be granted suppressing the publication of the appellant's article. It is of the utmost importance that the public know of his history of alcoholism if they are to make a fully informed decision as to whether or not he should be elected as their representative.

2.2 Freedom of Expression and the Politician

In *Lingens v Austria*[131] the ECHR imported a concept from the US Supreme Court that politicians must expect and tolerate greater public scrutiny and criticism than other citizens. It stressed the media's crucial role in reporting matters of public interest. Freedom of the press provided the public with "one of the best means of discovering and forming an opinion of the ideas and attitudes of political leaders"[132]. The court also stated that "[t]he limits of acceptable criticism are accordingly wider as regards a politician as such than as regards a private individual"[133]. In *Sunday Times v UK*[134] the ECHR said that the Freedom of Expression (Article 10) guarantee, not only includes "the freedom of the press to inform the public, but also the right of the public to be properly informed."[135] A person who is a recovering alcoholic and is standing for election, is placing himself in the public eye and presenting himself as a responsible and suitable person for public office. The public has a right to put him under thorough scrutiny as to his suitability for office.

2.3 Freedom of Expression and the Margin of Appreciation

The court's restriction of the margin of appreciation in relation to Article 10 was demonstrated in the *Spycatcher case*[136]. A distinction was drawn between two time periods before and after the controversial book was published in the US. In relation to the first time period it ruled that the injunctions against the publication were justified because of a risk that the material was prejudicial to the British Secret Service. In relation to the second period, the court ruled unanimously that Article 10 had been violated. The government's aim of protecting

---

131 Series A, No. 103; 8 EHHR 103 (1986).
132 Ibid at p 419.
133 Ibid.
134 Sunday Times v UK, Series A, No. 30; 2 EHHR 245.
135 Ibid p 277-282.
136 Observer and Guardian v UK, Series A, No 216; 14 EHHR 153.

confidentiality was no longer relevant as the information had entered the public domain. The court reiterated that freedom of expression is not to be balanced against other interests but is "subject to a number of exceptions which...must be narrowly interpreted"[137] The appellant's right to privacy was not breached as the article was no longer private. It had already been made available in the public library. The interests of the appellant in restricting the publication are not sufficient to meet the narrow limits of a permissible exception to the Article 10 right.

2.4 Freedom of Expression and Prior Censorship

The American Convention on Human Rights preserves a wide concept of freedom of expression protecting, not only the right to express thoughts but to receive information, to ensure the function of democracy and the free exchange of ideas in the public forum. The right "shall not be subject to prior censorship"[138]. This ensures that no preventative measures are used but only subsequent imposition of sanctions on those who are guilty of abuses.[139] An injunction against the respondent should not be granted, since the appellant has not made out a sufficient case at this interlocutory stage[140].

3   Copyright

3.1 Copyright as an Instrument of Censorship

Addressing the House of Commons in 1841 Macauley remarked as follows: "It is desirable that we should have a supply of good books: we cannot have such a supply unless men of letters are liberally remunerated: and the least objectionable way of remunerating them is by means of copyright."[141] Writing in the Columbia Law Review in 1945, Chafee described copyright as facilitating "the

---

137 Ibid.

138 Art 13(2) American Convention of Human Rights. Laddie J. one of the UK's leading intellectual property judges, has indicated the UK should consider adopting a more general defence.

139 Appeal to the Inter American Commission on Human Rights in the "Diplomatic Impunity" case, Report No. 11/96, case 11.230-Chile, May 3 1996

140 This presents a precedent for reducing the restriction of the Right to Freedom of Expression to the extent that no interlocutory procedures can be justified where this right is concerned.

141 Cited by Chafee "Reflections on the Law of Copyright I" (1945) 4 Columbia Law Review, 503 at p 507.

free flow of ideas and imaginative ideas across national boundaries".[142] Copyright was thus conceived as a means of promoting education and the exchange of information and ideas. Copyright was not intended to provide a vehicle for censorship and the suppression of information and this Court should not permit its abuse for that purpose.

3.2 Enforcement of Copyright Contrary to Public Policy/Interest

In *Glyn v Weston Feature Film Co.*[143] Younger J. held that copyright could not subsist in a "grossly immoral work". The House of Lords in *AG v Guardian Newspapers ("Spycatcher")*[144] indicated that the courts would not enforce a claim to copyright in a work where its publication was contrary to the public interest. This reflects a broader principle that copyright protection should be denied to those who seek to exercise it in a manner which clearly offends the public interest. In *Ashdown v Telegraph Group*[145] the Court of Appeal confirmed that the public interest could justify the publication of work against the wishes of the copyright-owner even in the absence of wrongdoing on his part. There is a strong public interest in revealing that the appellant who is so strongly opposed to alcohol consumption, was himself diagnosed as suffering from incipient alcoholism.

3.3 Fair Dealing

In *Ashdown v Telegraph Group* the Court of Appeal accepted that the most important factor relevant to the defence of fair dealing is whether the alleged infringer is commercially competing with the proprietor's exploitation of the copyright work. The court supported the view expressed in *Laddie, Prescott & Vitoria*[146] that where there is no competition the defence is likely to succeed "if the defendant's additional purpose is to right a wrong, to ventilate an honest grievance, to engage in political controversy...". The court accepted that the second most important factor is whether the work has already been published or otherwise exposed to the public and said that the defence is likely to fail where unpublished information has been obtained by some underhand

---

142 Ibid. at p 506.
143 [1916] 1 Ch. 261 at p 269.
144 [1990] 1 AC 109 at p 262, per Lord Keith.
145 [2002] Ch. 149 at p 173.
146 The Modern Law of Copyright and Designs (3rd Ed., 2000).

dealing. And finally the court identified the extent of the taking as being the third most important factor.

Whilst the respondent did publish the whole of the appellant's article, it was not competing with the appellant in any way and it did not deprive the appellant of any commercial benefit which he might otherwise have derived from that work. Moreover, the respondent was publishing a work which had previously been published with the consent of the appellant and which it obtained in a public library.

3.4 Copyright Interfering with Confidence

The law of confidence is concerned with striking an appropriate balance between free speech and privacy. This Court should not allow copyright to upset the careful balance established by the law of confidence.

4 Confidence

4.1 Information already in public domain and thus incapable of being protected

The status of information is a question of fact, not intention. If material is in fact in the public domain, it is irrelevant that the confider intended that it be kept secret. It is clear from *Mustad v Allcock and Dosen*[147] that once the disclosee publishes the information, the obligation of confidence comes to an end. Here, the information was freely accessible to the general public in a State library. That this was not intended by the appellant is irrelevant.

The degree of publication is relevant, but the publication here was more than sufficient. Indeed, Bently and Sherman[148] note in this regard that "[a]s Internet use grows, it will be increasingly difficult for a claimant to establish that information known in one place is confidential elsewhere".

AG v Guardian Newspapers[149] ("Spycatcher") is powerful authority for the respondent's case. In this decision, the House of Lords held that once information was in the public domain the courts could not restrain further publica-

---

147 (1928) [1963] 3 All ER 416. Cited by Bently and Sherman Intellectual Property Law (2001, OUP).
148 Bently and Sherman at p 929.
149 [1987] 1 WLR 1248.

tion, even if the information entered the public domain via a breach of confidence.

4.2 No Obligation on Respondent to Keep Information Confidential

Coco v Clark[150] requires that there exist on the part of the respondent an obligation to keep the information confidential. The parties in this case are not in any contractual or fiduciary relationship. The respondent was an indirect recipient of information and not party to any relationship of confidence. It is unreasonable to suggest that a person who came across information in a public library, freely available to the general public, was grossly negligent in failing to realise that a breach of confidence was involved, and this is the standard set down in *AG v Guardian Newspapers*. It is not sufficient to show that the failure to appreciate the confidential nature of the information was "merely careless, naïve or stupid" (*Thomas v Pearce*).[151]

4.3 Public Interest Defence

Wood V.-C. in *Gartside v Outram*[152] famously said: "there is no confidence as to the disclosure of iniquity". The case of *Initial Services v Putterill*[153] established that the concept of "iniquity" embraces not only crime or fraud, but any misconduct of such a nature that it is in the public interest to disclose it. This view was reasserted by Lord Denning in *Fraser v Evans*[154]. While it is generally accepted that a distinction must be drawn between information which is interesting to the public and information, the disclosure of which is in the public interest, this case is a clearly in the latter category. The appellant is seeking public office on a pledge of zero tolerance regarding drug and alcohol offences. Where a politician bases his campaign on a condemnation of certain practices, the public has an interest in knowing whether he has ever engaged in such practices himself. Such information is relevant to the public's assessment of the sincerity and the objectivity of the politician in adopting such an agenda.

---

150 [1968] FSR 415.
151 [2000] FSR 718. See also Shelley Films v Rex Features [1994] EMLR 134; (third party only on notice when must have seen signs specifically prohibiting taking of photographs); also Douglas v Hello [2001] FSR 732.
152 (1857) 26 LJ Ch 113
153 [1968] 1 QB 396
154 [1969] 1 All ER 8

Moreover, it is generally accepted by psychologists that alcoholics are never fully 'cured' of their affliction in the common sense of the word. Voters are entitled to be appraised of facts which may affect the ability of a politician to carry out his duties in public office.

Campbell v MGN[155] lends strong support to the respondent's claim. Here, it was held that the public interest defence operated to justify disclosure of the appellant's narcotic abuse. The appellant was a supermodel celebrity, with no professional responsibility to the public. *A fortiori*, the double standards and dishonesty of a potential public servant and MP deserve to be disclosed to the public so that they may make an informed choice in the parliamentary elections.

5   Interlocutory Injunctive Relief

The automatic grant of interim relief based on the test developed in *American Cyanamid v Ethicon*[156] would have grave implications for freedom of expression[157]. The dangers associated with such a policy have been recognised by the English legislature in the 1998 Human Rights Act which establishes that where the relief sought encroaches upon freedom of expression a claimant must show that there is more than a serious issue to be tried.

---

155 [2002] EWCA Civ 1373

156 [1975] AC 396

157 See Hubbard v Vosper [1972]; Cambridge Nutrition v BBC [1990]; Times v Mirror Group [1993] where the application of American Cyanamid was eschewed in favour of a more detailed examination of the merits of the parties' claims.

2003 IP MOOT (example 3—appellant's case)

On behalf of the appellant Mr Marco Polo, the following grounds of appeal are summarily submitted:

1 That there was copyright infringement of Mr Polo's 'For You Only' article as no license implied or otherwise was consented to Devil-May-Care (DMC) Internet Co. Ltd.

2 That there was breach of confidentiality.

3 That whilst Erewhon does not have a "a right to privacy" law, Art 8 of the European Convention of Human Rights allows the appellant protection as to respect to private life.

4 That the Freedom of Expression operated by the press and other tabloid entities does not afford them a free rein over an individual's private life.

These are explained fully below:

1 Lack Of Implied License:

The appellant submits that respondents could not have assumed an implied licence to copy the article in question.

There are three grounds for this submission:

1(1) A special relationship must exist between the parties in order for such a licence to be implied. (*Blair v Tomkins & Osbourne [1971] 2 QB 78*. Upon full payment an Architect does pass an implied license to the owners, purchasers, their surveyors and workmen (common custom of trade). It can be expected that the common custom of trade is for such copyright materials to be circulated by, and to, all those thus concerned in the final process: the erection of a building). No such relationship exists or existed between Mr Polo and DMC Internet Co Ltd or DMC Internet and AU.

1(2) An implied license can only arise if linked to an original purpose. (Reliance on *Stavin & Bradford v Volpoint Properties [1971] Ch 1007*. Held in the circumstances that there was no implied licence to use the architect's drawings for a purpose other than that which was intended, namely seeking planning permission.) Mr Polo's article was expressly licensed to AU for publication for the sole purpose of giving hope to, and aiding the recovery of other members of AU. Thus an implied licence cannot be relied upon by DMC as at no time was the purpose of said article to entertain the public through, or to facilitate an increase in internet traffic and business of, DMC's website.

1(3) An implied licence can only naturally flow from an express licence. (the case of *Nelson v Rye [1996] EMLR 37*. A music group manager sought to recover expenses from the profits the band had gained. Held that there had been no express agreement that R would have his expenses reimbursed and therefore no term to that affect would be implied.) As no express licence was granted to DMC to copy Mr Polo's article in the first place no licence can therefore be implied.

Example: Had AU also owned a website where it also posted articles of recovered members then it is reasonable to assume not only that express licence has been granted by Mr Polo for AU to copy the article for publication in its newsletter but also that should AU post the article on it's website AU can reasonably rely on an implied licence.

From the above submissions, having been indicated to satisfy the principles in the case law thus cited, the following conclusion is thus offered:

> That because DMC Internet was neither in the mind's of, or a party to the express licence granted by, Mr Polo to AU, DMC Internet cannot claim licence, implied or otherwise for their copying of the article within their website. Such copying is infringement of Mr Polo's copyright in the article.

Taking the above into consideration the appellant respectfully implores the Supreme Court of Erewhon to reverse the first holding of the High Court and find DMC Internet liable for infringement of copyright.

2   Breach of Confidence

The appellant submits that the facts of the case support, through the three part test of Megarry J in *Coco v AN Clarke (Engineers) Ltd [1969] RPC 41* p47 (as affirmed by the judgement of Lord Keith in *AG v Guardian Newspapers (No2) [1990] 1 AC 109*), the case that DMC was under an obligation of confidence and as such by their actions breached that confidence.

Key elements to be satisfied in accordance with the above:

2(1) The information must have the necessary quality of confidence about it. (Not in the public domain, not merely trivial).

Arguments in Support:

(a) Publication to a limited number of subscribers does not place the information in the public domain. (*Exchange Telegraph Co Ltd v Central News Ltd [1897] 2 Ch 48*).

(b) That 22 years had passed in the case before the Supreme Court supports the submission that the information is not currently in the public domain. (*AG v Guardian Newspapers (No2) [1990]*)

(c) That the information is not trivial (mere 'tittle-tattle'). That an individuals past history with alcoholism and treatment thereof, represents clearly a sensitive and personal, thus justifiably confidential, part of that individuals life. (*Stephens v Avery [1988] Ch 449*), (*Barrymore v News Group Newspapers Ltd [1997] FSR 600*).

(d) Prior disclosure to a limited number of people will not necessarily rob the information of its confidentiality. (*AG v Guardian Newspapers (No2) [1990]*).

2(2) The information itself must have been imparted in circumstances where the confidant ought reasonably to have known that the information had been imparted in confidence.

Arguments in Support:

a) Limited Purpose Test. That the information was communicated for a limited purpose only and any such deviation from the purpose signifies a breach. (*Saltman Engineering Co Ltd v Campbell Engineering Co Ltd [1963] 3 All ER 413n*), (*Ackroyds (London) Ltd v Islington Plastics [1962] RPC 97*).

Limited purpose test is objective: is not necessary to show that the respondent *knew* that the information imparted was for a limited purpose. It is only necessary to show that, given the circumstances in which the information was imparted, the respondent ought to have known. (*Smith Kline & French Laboratories (Australia) v Secretary Department of Community Services and Health (1990) 22 FC 73*).

b) A Special Relationship or communication between the appellant and respondent was not necessary in establishing an obligation of confidence. (Lord Goff: *AG v Guardian Newspapers (No2) [1990]*), *(Stephens v Avery [1988]), (Francrome v Mirror Group Newspapers [1984]), (Shelly Films v Rex Features Ltd [1994]), (Creation Records Ltd v News Group Newspapers Ltd [1997]).*

2(3) The last, and somewhat lesser, test is that there must be an unauthorised use of the confidential information to the detriment of the party that communicated it.

Arguments submitted in support:

a) For the reasons already given—lack of licence implied or otherwise; that the information was used by DMC for a purpose other than which it was intended—it is submitted that there was an unauthorised use of the confidential information.

b) That as such Mr Polo suffered detriment in the way of shock and fears further detriment considering the appellant's political position and political stances. (Lord Keith in *AG v Guardian Newspapers (No2) [1990]*)

From the above submissions, having been indicated to satisfy the principles in *Coco v AN Clarke*, the following conclusion is thus offered:

> That Mr Polo's article indeed possessed the necessary quality of confidence, that in DMC Internet indirectly coming into possession of the article was such imparted with an obligation of confidence, that in displaying the article within its website did so unauthorised as to cause detriment to the appellant, leading to the breach of said confidence.

For these reasons the appellant implores the Supreme Court of Erewhon to reverse the second holding of the High Court and find DMC Internet liable for breach of confidentiality.

3. Right to Privacy

It has been noted by the appellant that the Supreme Court of Erewhon will normally treat the European Convention of Human Rights (ECHR) provisions as part of the law of Erewhon, as such the appellant respectfully reminds the Supreme Court the following:

3(1) (a) It is clear that Art 10 (Freedom of expression, which will be looked at below) can be actionable between private individuals.

(b) Whilst the respondents argue protection under Art 10, under subsection 2 of the article certain qualifications must be adhered to, namely:

"The exercise of the these freedoms (expression), since it carries with it duties and responsibilities, may be subject to such formalities, conditions, restrictions or penalties as are proscribed by law and are necessary...for the protection of the reputation or rights of others, for preventing the disclosure of information received in confidence..."

(c) Since Art 10.2 is so qualified it is necessary to have regard for Art 8 Respect for Family and Private Life.

(d) In submission the qualification allows the court to not only adopt the ECHR Right of Privacy in the absence of any equivalent national provision, but also to superimpose such a right as being actionable between private parties.

(e) The above thereby ensures a state maintains its positive obligations to protect the rights and freedoms of its citizens arising from **Art 1 ECHR**.

Case submitted in support of the above assertions:

3(2) *Douglas and Others v Hello! Ltd [2001] 2 WLR 992,*

Mills (Heather) v News Group Newspapers Ltd [2001] EMLR 41,

Campbell (Naomi) v Mirror Group Newspapers Ltd [2002] EWCA Civ 1373 CA.

The following conclusion is thus submitted:

> It is submitted that in the light of, the above recent, case law authority and by virtue of statutory interpretation, a Right of Privacy can exist in Erewhon and as such can be used to protect Mr Polo (a private individual) against intrusion by DMC Internet (a private party).

As such the appellant requests the Supreme Court to reverse the third holding as found by the High Court.

4. DMC Internet's Freedom Of Expression

As has been indicated above whilst DMC Internet may seek protection under such an ECHR provision, the provision itself must be qualified. In so doing then a balancing exercise will normally be adopted. In this case then does the Public Interest in publicising the article outweigh the protection that must be afforded the appellant on the grounds of Right to privacy?

4(1) It is submitted that there can be no public interest in reporting an intimate and private episode that occurred before Mr Polo entered the media spotlight. The events are not indicative of Mr Polo at present, and such reporting does nothing more than unnecessarily intrude upon Mr Polo's past.

(Cited in comparison: *Reynolds (Albert) v Times Newspapers Ltd & Others [1998] 3 WLR 862).*

4(2) There can be no public interest in reporting events that have not been previously misrepresented. The events concerning alcoholism did not occur whilst Mr Polo was a politician, and thus requires no record to be put straight by the media or indeed facilitates any debate as to Mr Polo's fitness for office.

(Cited in comparison: *Campbell (Naomi) v Mirror Group Newspapers Ltd [2002] EWCA Civ 1373 CA).*

4(3) Merely because an individual has achieved a high status, does not mean the media have a free reign over that individual's private life. To allow such a reign would destroy all and any right of privacy.

(Cited in support: *Douglas and Others v Hello! Ltd [2001] 2 WLR 992*).

In conclusion to the above submissions the following is put forth:

> The appellant submits that to uphold the forth holding of the High Court would be to destroy the appellants right to all privacy, be it past, present, future, during prominence or before. To uphold the ruling would be to suggest that merely because the public might find interesting what Mr Polo was like 22 years ago, would be to contravene those media qualifications as set out in Art 10 (2) concerning reputation, confidence and thus the appellants privacy.

The appellant would again implore the court, in taking into consideration the above, to find that DMC Internet, in displaying the article, cannot be afforded protection under Art 10 ECHR Freedom of expression.

2003 IP MOOT (example 3—respondent's case)

EXAMPLE THREE—RESPONDENT'S CASE—IP MOOT 2003

IN THE SUPREME COURT OF EREWHON

In the Case of

Marco Polo
> Appellant

v

Devil-May-Care Internet Co
> Respondent

Respondent's Written Pleadings

1. In response to an appeal by Marco Polo, from the decision of the Erewhon Court of Appeal, the Respondent submits the following pleadings.

2. As the English State has incorporated the European Convention on Human Rights into its domestic law, it is expedient to rely on English law as persuasive authority, particularly as English is the language of Erewhon.

3. With regard to point of appeal "A)", the Respondent argues that by expressly licensing AU to publish his article, the Appellant impliedly licensed the public at large to use his account of his drink problem—Blair v Tomkins & Osbourne (1971) 2 QB 78, Nelson v Rye (1996) EMLR 37.

4. This implied license satisfies the criterion in Stavin & Bradford v Volpoint Properties (1971) Ch 1007, that an implied license can only arise where it is linked to the original purpose of the copyright material. This, it is submitted, is because the article was written with the intention of engaging an indeterminately large section of the public.

5. In respect of point of appeal "B)", the Respondent contends that the three requisite elements identified in Coco v Clark [1969] RPC 41 for an actionable claim are not present. Consequently, the information in question did not possess "the necessary quality of confidence about it", was not

"imparted in circumstances importing an obligation of confidence" and there was no "unauthorised use of that information to the detriment of the party communicating it"—Saltman v Campbell (1948) 65 RPC 203 as per Lord Greene MR.

6. These three points are examined respectively forthwith.

7. It is contended that by publishing the article in question in a newsletter to be circulated, the Claimant rendered it "public property" irrespective of the fact that unbeknownst to him or the persons in charge of the support group, the newsletter was made accessible to the general public via a library. Furthermore, although it could be argued that the information was circulated around too specific a group of people (i.e. alcoholics) to be classified as being in the "public domain", the judgement in Ryan v Capital Leasing [1998] EIPR 93 which dictates that where "the information is well known to that section of the public which has an interest in knowing the information it is in the public domain". If it transpires that the group of people in question constitute too specific a group, the fact that the information in question was still available in the library remains unaltered, thus placing AU in a more liable position than the respondent.

8. It was confirmed in Albert v Strange (1849) 2 DeG & Sm 652 that it suffices that any confidential information be merely 'relatively secret'. However, the aforementioned case can be distinguished from the present case, in that the former concerned individuals who were already personally proximate to the claimant.

9. It is contended that the Claimant and the Respondent (being strangers) lack the close proximity of relationship requisite for a direct duty of confidentiality to arise.

10. In the event that a duty owed by the Respondent to the Claimant is established, the respondent is still availed by the fact that he acted legally in obtaining the information; he does not therefore come under any obligation of confidence. This is confirmed in Malone v Commissioner of Metropolitan Police [1979] 1 Ch 344.

11. Furthermore, following from the judgement in Attorney General v Guardian (No 2) [1990] AC 109 that "a duty of confidence arises where confidential information comes to the knowledge of a person in circumstances where he has notice or is held to have agreed that the information

is confidential..." it is contended that as such has not occurred, the Respondent must be under no such obligation.

12. The article itself, is an explicit account of the Claimant's personal experience of 'incipient alcoholism'. At present the Claimant is a candidate for Parliament. It is conceivable that the disclosure of personal information of such a nature could damage the Claimant's chances of success. However, it is equally conceivable that the Claimant will win admiration with the public on account of overcoming his alcoholism. The question as to whether the Claimant has suffered detriment is therefore uncertain.

13. With regard to points of appeal "C)" and "D)", the following is submitted.

14. The obligation conferred (upon "public authorities" of contracting states) by Article 8 of the European Convention on Human Rights, to refrain from interfering with individuals' right to respect for their private lives is not contended.

15. Prima facie, Article 8 only applies in respect of public authorities. This appears to preclude in the present case, an inference that adherence to the Convention necessitates a recognition of a "right of privacy" in contracting states.

16. The Respondent concedes that Article 1 of the Convention appears to confer a positive obligation upon contracting states, to enforce Article 8 in respect of private individuals.

17. However, much importance should be placed on the Article 8 phrase "public authority"; a purposive construction clearly reveals that the right to respect for private and family life was intended, by the Convention's draftsmen, to be qualified, to have direct effect only in respect of public authorities—the Article 1 requirement that all Convention rights be secured, being intended to be implemented by individual contracting states, as this is a dispute between private individuals.

18. Furthermore, a substantive "right of privacy" is not recognised in English Law. English case law demonstrates that the law of confidence sufficiently encompasses the (contended) right to privacy: Douglas v Hello! (2001) EMLR 1, Venables v News Group Newspapers (2001) EMLR 10, Campbell v MGN Ltd (2003 EMLR 2), WB v H Bauer Publishing limited (2002) EMLR 8.

19. It follows that a judgement in favour of the Respondent with regard to point of appeal "B)", will satisfy point C).

20. The aforementioned case law also demonstrates the conflict between Article 8 of the Convention and Article 10, which guarantees freedom of expression.

21. The approach of the European Court of Human Rights, to this matter manifestly favours freedom of information in the press: Sunday Times v UK (1979) EHRR 245, particularly where the integrity of politicians is scrutinised: Lingens v Austria (1986) 8 EHRR 407.

22. A distinction of substance cannot be made between a newspaper and the Respondent's website—the purpose of both is to convey information. Any differences of style are superficial.

23. Counsel would accordingly implore the Court to rule in the Respondent's favour and dismiss this appeal.

2003 MOCK TRIAL—Music or Silence?

Zen-inspired composer, C Hopin, arduously laboured over the creation of the musical score '360 seconds'…of silence.

London-based band, The Electric Nuns, allegedly copied the score in their track '90 and a bell' but claimed it has never heard of Hopin's silent work.

The Mock Trial, presented by Oxford Intellectual Property Research Centre, took place in May 2003 The cast of characters were:-

Judge: The Honourable Justice Robin Jacob.
Counsel for Claimant: Mr. Michael Silverleaf QC
Counsel for Defendant: Mr. Henry Carr QC
Claimant: "Mr. Hopin", Mr. Harry Small, Baker & Mackenzie Solicitors
Defendant: Sally Airie, Ms. Anna Edwards-Stuart, Baker & Mackenzie Solicitors.

Particulars of Claim

1. The Claimant is an internationally renowned composer and recording artiste of original music. The claimant is the author and proprietor of an original copyright musical work entitled "360 seconds", (The Piece).

   Particulars of Creation and Ownership.

   The Claimant is, and was at all material times, a United Kingdom citizen. The Claimant composed the Piece in or about November 1977.

2. The Defendant is a rock musician. From a date unknown to the Claimant, but no later than January 2002, the Defendant has recorded and produced for sale and sold to the public copies of an album entitled "Rockin' Rev", ("the Album"). Amongst the tracks contained on the Album is one entitled "90 ans a bell" ("the Track"). The Track reproduces the whole or a substantial part of the Piece.

An example of the Album complained of was obtained by solicitors for the Claimant from Tower Records in Picadilly Circus, London on the 11th of January 2002. The album sleeve notes state "All tracks written and produced by Sally Arie." The credits for the Track state, "(Arie/Hopin)". A copy of the said album is available from the Claimant's solicitors upon reasonable notice.

3. In the premises, the Defendant has infringed the Claimant's copyright in the Claimant's Piece by copying or causing to be copied, issuing or causing to be issued to the public the Track which is a whole or substantial copy of the Piece.

4. Further or in the alternative, the Track is a derogatory treatment of the Piece in that the Track distorts and/or mutilates the Piece and/or is prejudicial to the honour of and/or the reputation of the Claimant.

5. Further or in further alternative, the Track falsely attributes its composition to the Claimant as joint author with the Defendant.

PARTICULARS

Pending disclosure of documents and/or the obtaining of further information during the course of proceedings the Claimant will rely in support of this allegation on the facts and matters pleaded in paragraph 2 above and in particular the Defendant's reference to the Claimant in the sleeve notes to the Album.

1. By reason of the matters aforesaid, the Defendant has acted in flagrant disregard of the Claimant's rights. The Claimant is entitled to additional statutory damages under section 97(2) of the Copyright, Designs and Patents Act 1988 due to the flagrancy of the infringements and the benefits thus accruing to the Defendant. Pending disclosure of documents and/or the obtaining of further information during the course of proceedings the Claimant will rely in support of this allegation on the facts and matters referred to in paragraph 2 hereunder. In particular, reliance is placed on the Defendant's acknowledgement of the copying in the sleeve notes.

2. By reason of the Defendant's acts complained of, the Claimant has suffered loss and damage. The Defendant threatens and intends to continue the activities complained of, whereby the Claimant will continue to suffer loss and damage.

3. The foregoing comprise the best particulars the Claimant is presently able to give of the Defendant's wrongful acts. The Claimant will rely upon and seek relief in respect of all such acts that come to light.

4. The claimant is entitled to and claims interest pursuant to section 35A of the Supreme Court Act 1981 alternatively under the equitable jurisdiction of this Honourable Court.

AND the Claimant claims:

(1) An injunction restraining the Defendant, (whether acting by himself or by other acting on her behalf, on her instructions or with her encouragement or otherwise howsoever) from:

    a.   infringing the Claimant's copyright in the Piece;

    b.   infringing the Claimant's moral rights in the Piece.

(2) An order for delivery up, alternatively obliteration on oath, of all articles in the possession, custody or control of the Defendant, the sale or use of which articles would contravene the foregiong injunction;

(3) An inquiry as to damages suffered by the Claimant alternatively at the Claimant's option on account of the profits accruing to the Defendant by reason of the acts of copyright infringement and infringement of moral rights together with an order that the Defendant do pay to the claimant such sum as may be found due upon the taking of such inquiry or account together with interest thereon pursuant to section 35A of the Supreme Court Act 1981, alternatively the equitable jurisdiction of the Honourable Court.

(4) Costs;

(5) Further or other relief.

THE DEFENCE'S RESPONSE

1. Paragraph references are references to paragraph numbers in the Particulars of Claim unless otherwise stated. The Defendant adopts the abbreviations used in the Particulars of Claim.

2. It is denied that the Piece is a musical work. The purported work is alleged to consist of silence, which is the absence of noise. There is no tonal variation of any kind within the piece. Accordingly, the Piece is not a musical

work within the meaning of section 3(1) of the Copyright, Designs and Patents Act 1988.

3. Further or in the alternative, it is denied that the Piece has been recorded in writing or otherwise. The absence of something cannot be recorded.

4. Further, or in the alternative, it is denied that the Piece is an original work. The Piece is a copy of Rauschenberg's "White Picture" ("The Picture"). A copy of the Picture is attached to this Defence.

5. Save as aforesaid, paragraph 1 is admitted.

6. It is denied that the Track reproduces any part of the Piece. The Track is not silent, it includes background noise and a deliberate noise in the form of an electronic chime, after approximately 58 seconds. Save as aforesaid, parafraph 2 is admitted.

7. In the premises, paragraph 3 and 4 are denied.

8. If, which is denied, the Track is a whole or substantial copy of the Piece, it is denied that it is derogatory treatment of the Piece.

9. It is denied that the Claimant is attributed as a composer of the Track. The reference to the Claimant is an acknowledgement of the lineage of the Track and not an indication of authorship. Paragraph 5 is denied.

10. It is denied that the Claimant has suffered loss and damage whether as a result of the Defendant's actions or at all. It is denied that the Claimant is entitled to the relief or any relief.

WITNESS STATEMENT OF CHARLES HOPIN

I CHARLES HOPIN of 13 Berkley Square, Chelsea, London SW5 0PJ will say as follows:

1. I have been a professional composer since graduating from the Royal Academy of Music in 1970. I have composed a large number of pieces for a variety of instruments and in a variety of styles. I am perhaps best known for my piano compositions "Song of the Dark Island", "Too many cooks", and the score for the film "Hoopla Hoopla Hoopla".

2. I am the composer of '360 seconds'. I composed the piece in 1977. It was first performed at The Artists' Welfare Fund Benefit Concert, Woodstock, New York, on the 12th of February 1978 by the pianist Arthur Willams. It has subsequently been performed a number of times.

3. '360 seconds' is often referred to as my silent piece. However, I do not believe that there is such a thing as a total absence of sound. I recall visiting an anechoic chamber at Harvard University in 1976. I expected to hear nothing but in fact heard two sounds, one high and one low—my nervous system and my blood circulating. I conclude that try as we might to make silence we cannot.

4. The genesis of '360 seconds' was a long and difficult process. In total it took me two years of preparation and drafts. I was concerned that it would be taken as a joke and a renounciation of work, whereas, I also knew that if it was done it would be the highest form of work. In particular, I did not want to appear foolish or worse yet shock or insult my audience.

5. A significant influence on my work was the revelation that the purpose of music is to quiet the mind. Prior to composition of '360 seconds' I had immersed myself in the writings of various Zen masters. In particular I consulted the I Ching about the relationship between even and uneven numbers. Through coin tosses, I received the answer that exclusively even numbers should appear.

6. I created 6 charts for durations. Within each chart there are sixty four elements (since silence also has a length). Through the use of fractions measured following a standard scale (2.5 cm equals a crochet), these durations are, for the purposes of musical compositions, practically infinite in number. Consulting the chart and using only the even numbers it became apparent that this meant: no tones.

7. The piece consists of four 90-second movements. Each of the movements appears in manuscript form as a typewritten score which lists the movements with Roman Numerals and the word TACET, ("silent"), below each of the movements. Below this appears the following passage:

"The title of this work is the total length in seconds of its performance. At Woodstock, NY, 12th February 1978 by Arthur Williams, pianist, who indicated at the start of each movement by opening the keyboard lid and the end of each movement by closing the keyboard lid. However, the work may be performed by (any) instrumentalist or combination of instrumentalists and be repeated any number of times.

8. I did refer to the Rauschenberg painting "White Picture" during the creation of "360 seconds". Its absence of colour or shading of any kind combined with the fact that it was nonetheless very expressive was inspiring to

me. It is not however, comparable to my work, which aims to collect all sounds into the music. By contrast, the white painting is a rejection of form and expression.

9. In January 2002, I was informed by the Performing Rights Society that Ms Sally Arie had produced an album, "Rockin Rev" by the band "The Electric Nuns". The album included a track entitled "90 and a bell". I have listened to the track which consists of 90 seconds of recording and at approximately 58 seconds there can be heard the sound of an electric chime which lasts for about two seconds. During the 90 seconds vague background noises can be heard, which have been picked up by the microphone. I believe the hum of air-conditioning can be distinguished. It is unclear whether the electric chime is a deliberate introduction or merely a particularly distinct piece of background noise.

10. In essence, the work exactly reproduces the spirit of '360 seconds'. Indeed, Ms Arie acknowledges the connection because the sleeve notes state that the composition of "90 and a bell" is by Arie/Hopin.

11. The reproduction of my work on this album of rock music denegrates the important artistic statement that I was attempting to make in my original composition. The aggressive nature of the electric chime is discordant and unattractive to the ear and the implication that I would have co-operated in the composition of the track is something I deeply resent.

12. My solicitors wrote to Ms Arie, but despite the clear abduction of my work, Ms Arie refused to provide recompense for the taking of my efforts. I was left with no alternative than to commence proceedings.

TRANSCRIPT OF THE MOCK TRIAL "MUSIC OF SILENCE", AS PERFORMED.

<u>Michael Silverleaf, QC, for Claimant</u>: Has your Lordship had opportunity to read the papers? Look at the claim.

It it about 4 movements of 90 seconds each. The claim is that the defendant has made derogatory treatment of the Claimant's piece and has made a false attribution to her own music piece.

Miss Sally Airie expressed her music piece to be attributed to Mr. Hopin.

WE state that there is no such thing as silence. If you put a sea-shell up to your ear to demonstrate the sound of the sea, we know that what you hear is not the sound of the sea. What you hear is the sound of your blood pulsing in your ear. My point is that this example acts as a reminder that there is no such thing as silence.

The Right Honourable Justice Robin Jacob Judge: But this sound is not created by your client, is it?

Michael Silverleaf for Claimant: The object of Mr Hopin's piece is to listen to it and to appreciate; it brings the natural sound around aware to you.

Robin Jacob Judge: What about the sound around of a pneumatic drill? Does that make you appreciate?

Michael Silverleaf, QC: Yes, but the sound of a pneumatic drill is deliberately created noise. What Miss Airie the defendant has done is that she has developed the whole of the claimant's piece. Therefore she is copying his piece. It is derogatory treatment of Mr Hopin's piece because it is introducing the conception of deliberately created noise, ie the bell. This damages the fabric of Mr Hopin's work. The fabric of Mr Hopin's work is the background natural sounds.

Your Lordship, I would now run briefly through the legal issues. This is my bundle consisting of the Copyright Act's relevant extractions.

Your Lordship, this is an unusual work; it involves the act of music; it consists of music. The definition of a musical work is in section 3(1) of the Act. It consists of music because it consists of musicians waiting in the background.

Robin Jacob Judge: Musical, how is it musical? It has no character. Then jukeboxes can be a musical work?

Michael Silverleaf for Claimant: Exactly.

Henry Carr, QC, for Defendant: The Piece of Mr Hopin was copied from the "White Painting". So it cannot be copyright.

<u>Michael Silverleaf for the Claimant</u>: He did not copy the "white painting". It is in an entirely different medium. It is of a different nature. Hopin's work is a period of time. Although the idea may spring from the "white painting", his piece was only inspired by the "white painting".

Also, the two things, the painting and the music, work in a different way. The object of the painting is to cause the viewer to see things that are not there. The piece "360 seconds" causes the listener to engage in what is already there. It has sufficient material to constitute a protected musical work. Look at an example.

The other evening, I attended a concert at the Barbican to listen to Mozart, Stravinsky and Benjamin Britten. Benjamin Britten's work is truly modern and without a pattern; just when you think you can begin to discern a pattern it changes completely. But there can be no doubt that Britten's work is a work of music.

<u>Robin Jacob Judge</u>: So what is the difference between music and noise?

<u>Michael Silverleaf for Claimant</u>: One is pre-ordained and the other isn't but the answer is that music is what the composer intends. There is no question of complexity of content.

(the <u>Northrop</u> case, pages 68 & 69—Definition of "drawing".)

"If simplicity were a disqualification........." This case has stood the test of time for 30 years.

<u>Robin Jacob Judge</u>: Suppose there were 10 notes and you take them away—this is not a musical work, is it?

<u>Michael Silverleaf for Claimant</u>: No. But as in a literary work, there is a boundary between something that is presented as a literary work and mere conversation. Mere conversation is not a literary work.

The defendant describes her work as cutting edge. Both her work and Mr Hopin 360 seconds piece are of natural sound. But WE say that Mr Hopin's work has sufficient originality to be protected. (sections 16 (1)(a) and 16 (3) and 17(2)).

<u>Robin Jacob Judge</u>: It boils down to whether it has been copied.

<u>Michael Silverleaf for Claimant</u>: The defendant intended to DRAW ON the work; she took exactly what Mr Hopin had created and added something to it. That must constitute a substantial part of her work and is worth protecting. (section 84—false attribution of work).

<u>Robin Jacob Judge</u>: But it reads as though Hopin is co-author. Does the work have to be a copyright work?

<u>Michael Silverleaf for Claimant</u>: Section 84 does not address this. Copyright entitles you to disassociate yourself to a particular work. (<u>Noah's article</u>). What is to be identified as the relevant work? The last 17 words were not his, therefore he could complain about the last seventeen words. Therefore it is not necessary that what is added can make it a different work. It is quite clear that the work is distorted, therefore it is derogatory. Therefore we seek damages for deliberate breach of claimant's rights; Miss Airie the defendant acknowledged Mr Hopin's work. I will now call my witness Mr Hopin.

<u>Michael Silverleaf for Claimant</u>: Mr Hopin, do you have copy of Court papers? Look at pages 12 to 15. Do you recognise this? Are the Contents true?

<u>Harry Small as Mr Hopin</u>:

Yes.

(Talks about his inspiration for his work as being through Zen thinking and years of thought).

<u>Henry Carr for Defendant</u>: Mr Hopin, you explain 360 seconds creation and said that it was a long and difficult process.

<u>Harry Small as Mr Hopin</u>: Yes, I drew on Zen philosophy for inspiration. I also received influences from tossing coins and Tarot readings. I had space for reflection.

Henry Carr for Defendant: These 8 charts of duration. You made this up for the purpose of the case, didn't you?

Harry Small as Mr Hopin: No. And the score gives direction to the musician. If they didn't have instruments they would not be performing my work. Beethoven has a rest in his 1st Movement (Beethoven's 5th Symphony).

Henry Carr for Defendant: But your 360 seconds piece had a rest but with no music either side of your rest. Our conclusion was, try as we might, we cannot make silence.

Harry Small as Mr Hopin: My piece's aim was to create a space for the absence of silence.

Henry Carr for Defendant: So your piece was to that the audience heard no music but will become aware of the exclusion of all background noise.

Harry Small as Mr Hopin: The piece itself does not contain silence.

Henry Carr for Defendant: Miss Airie's idea was to compose a piece in which distortion between natural noise and deliberate noise would be blurred. This was different to your single piece.

Harry Small as Mr Hopin: In my work there is true background noise.

Henry Carr for Defendant: Your silence is 6 minutes and hers is 90 seconds.

Harry Small as Mr Hopin: Mine is 90 seconds times four. The audience was expected to have done proper research before they came to my concerts. There are four distinct periods of 90 seconds of silence.

Henry Carr for Defendant: If I refer you to the "white painting". The thought you had was that if people paid money for a painting where there was no picture, they would also pay for a piece where there was no music? My client Miss

Airie had sold one million copies of her records; she was a successful rock musician, do you agree?

Harry Small as Mr Hopin: Yes

Henry Carr for Defendant: Since you sued the rock musician Miss Airie, you have become famous?

Harry Small as Mr Hopin: Yes; I have had Hello magazine interview me at my home.

Henry Carr for Defendant: You claim that Miss Airie's work was prejudicial to your honour and reputation. But previous to this case, you had none.

Harry Small as Mr. Hopin: I had my ZEN.

Henry Carr for Defendant: My client Miss Airie acknowledged that she was influenced by your work, even though she did not ever hear it.

Harry Small as Mr Hopin: I don't believe it.

Henry Carr for Defendant: What are you expecting to get in damages??
Hundred of thousands of pounds?

Harry Small as Mr Hopin: Yes.

Sally Airie—Ms. Anne Edwards-Stuart (Baker & Mackenzie solicitors) sworn in as witness:

Henry Carr for Defence: Is this your statement, Ms Arie? Can you confirm the accuracy of it?

Michael Silverleaf for Claimant: You find pop music more to your liking, do you not Ms Airie?

Sally Airie: Yes.

Michael Silverleaf for Claimant: You have composed the tracks in your first and second album, did you not? Did you compose the track 90 and the bell?

Sally Airie: Yes, I did.

Michael Silverleaf for Claimant: 90 refers to 90 seconds, does it? Did you write this?

Sally Airie: Yes I did.

Michael Silverleaf for Claimant: Were you aware of Hopin's work?

Sally Airie: Yes, I read an article.

Michael Silverleaf for Claimant: The conception was to bring natural background noise, was it? Was it to make the listener sit up and take notice?

Sally Airie: Yes, I was aware that it was going to make people think.

Micheal Silverleaf for Claimant: You took that conception from 360 seconds, didn't you?

Sally Airie: Yes.

Michael Silverleaf for Claimant: The idea was to make the listener sit up, wasn't it?

<u>Sally Airie</u>: Yes.

<u>Michael Silverleaf for Claimant</u>: The work itself was a period of silence interrupted with a single ring of a bell, was it?

<u>Sally Airie</u>: You have to be able to hear it.

<u>Michael Silverleaf for Claimant</u>: The listener has to understand that the surrounding silence is an integral part of the work. This conception was drawn from Hopin's work, wasn't it?

<u>Sally Airie</u>: Yes, but you see, the point of my piece is, is it supposed to be there or is it not supposed to be there? You have to hear the phone or bell.

<u>Michael Silverleaf for Claimant</u>: The idea was to integrate Hopin's work, wasn't it?

<u>Sally Airie</u>: Yes.

<u>Michael Silverleaf for Claimant</u>: By naming Hopin you intended to show where the work came from. And you attributed him as a joint composer?

<u>Sally Airie</u>: I was recognising that he had provided me with inspiration.

<u>Michael Silverleaf for Claimant</u>: You added a single bell noise to his piece of silence, didn't you? The reality is that you took the whole of Hopin's work and added a chime, isn't it?

<u>Sally Airie</u>: Yes, but I didn't deliberately do that.

<u>Henry Carr for Defendant</u>: A blank notebook is not a literary work. It is not a copyright work. A blank canvas is not an artistic work.

Robin Jacob Judge: Is silence the canvas of the composer?

Henry Carr for Defendant: Yes.

Look at the British Northrop case. The Vice Chancellor pointed out that if something is so barren (such as a straight line), it is not an artistic work. Similarly a blank silence is not an artistic work. Section 3(2) Copyright Designs and Patents Act 1988 does not subsist. A work must be capable of being recorded. Silence cannot be recorded. This is a charade, this piece by Hopin.

Robin Jacob Judge: But your client says this is a musical work?

Henry Carr for Defendant: She may be wrong. She is a witness. It is a question of legal policy. Her work contains silence, a bell and then silence. Counsel for Claimant said that Ms Airie had caused derogatory treatment of Mr Hopin's work because it is introducing a conception of deliberately created noise. But Mr Hopin made up the story about his creative processes. This must be taken into account. Further, we say that if there is no copyright, then the case ends here. The moral right, the right of eternity is not intended to create copyright. Look at section 77—moral rights. Section 77 is about the author of a copyright.

Robin Jacob Judge: If Hopin's work is copyright, then there is an infringement.

Henry Carr for Defendant: But in THIS case there has to be reproduction. Reproduction has to be very precise. Here, instead of complete silence, you have a work of constant noise. It externalises the background noise. Also, you are looking at a work of six minutes compared to Mr Hopin's work of one and a half minutes. If there is to be an infringement of copyright, there has to be precise reproduction. This section 77 does not say that the treatment must be derogatory. It is not like defamation. It is not a distortion. It is just different. When cross-examined, Mr Hopin made it clear that he is an unsuccessful composer and that he wanted to publicise his work. As to the allegation of misrepresentation, Ms Airie felt it the right thing to do to acknowledge her inspiration. We say that Mr Hopin has not been identified as the author, his name on the sleeve as co-author is just an acknowledgement of inspiration. Mr Hopin should get no damages.

Michael Silverleaf for Claimant: Mr Hopin is a serious classical composer. He has a lovely house that attracted Hello magazine who ran an article on it.

Robin Jacob Judge: He may have inherited it ; he did not gain it from his composition.

Michael Silverleaf for Claimant: The address of the defendant is based on false foundation. The whole basis of the case is that Ms Sally Airie's piece consists of a background to silence; it is the antithesis of silence. The background noise comes to the fore and forces the audience to participate in it. Clearly it is a work capable of being reproduced. As to the matter of money, My Lord, there is section 77—entitlement to be acknowledged and section 80 regarding derogatory treatment and section 84—false attribution. False attribution is a right of a different nature; it does not depend on the work.

Background noise is an essential part of Mr Hopin's work. This work of Sally Airie's is no different. She has appropriated the whole of Mr Hopin's work.

Robin Jacob Judge: This is a dispute between two deeply unattractive characters. The Plaintiff claims to be a composer; until this case, his work was arcane. He claims infringement of copyright of his 360 seconds piece of music, as he calls it. The score consists of nothing. The legal issue is whether Mr. Hopin's work is an original musical work.

1. Is it a musical work?

2. Is it original?

The Copyright Act does not describe musical work any further.

The Act says there shall be no copyright. The fact is that silence is not music and the way the claimant puts his case is that the purpose of his piece is that you can hear other things. Silence is just silence. The court did not understand his Zen either. I heard from the claimant his explanation as to how he devised his work. What he said in the witness statement is not what he said in the witness box.

The next question is, is it original? Has there been infringement? What the defendant did was that she had heard of this construct and put the 90 seconds of silence into her work and then put the noise of a bell in. She put it forward as if it was a serious proposition. I think she did it for the publicity and was very successful. Both parties did it for the publicity. The 360 seconds piece was divided into four parts of 90 seconds. Should anyone who had heard of Mr Hopin's work and kept quiet be an infringer?

Another way to look at it, if it is a work, is that it is of immense publicity.

If it is an original copyright work there is an element of infringement.

For false attribution of authorship, the work must be copyright work. If it was copyright, and I do not think it is, it is not derogatory.

Hopin's work had no reputation. The evidence seems to be that he publicised this case (Hello magazine article, etc). Therefore it is entirely untrue that his work was made derogatory.

As to the matter of authorship, the defendant put forward that this was composed by her and that she wanted to acknowledge Hopin's work which she heard of and which was an inspiration.

She did not tell the truth. It is self-evident that she acknowledged him as joint co-author. Therefore there has been no infringement and there is to be no damages awarded to Mr Hopin.

The truth is that nothing shall come of nothing. Silence is silence. Silence is not golden.

Michael Silverleaf for Claimant: My Lord, will you confirm that Mr Hopin's piece is not a work and that there has not been false attribution?

Henry Carr for Defendant: My Lord, will you clarify what you said about both the claimant and the defendant were "deeply unattractive" characters?

Robin Jacob Judge: Not faces, just characters.

Henry Carr for Defendant: Will you give the basis of indemnity costs? This case was sought to be supported by facts which you found to be untrue.

Micheal Silverleaf for Claimant: A plague of both of them! My Lord, permission to Appeal? There are important points of law here. It is a matter for Appeal. The case is sufficiently important to go to Appeal. It raises fundamental issues of the nature of copyright.

Robin Jacob Judge: I give my permission. As to the question of costs, the Court of Appeal will also look at the question of costs.

SHORT ESSAY:
THE MUSIC OF SILENCE

The Music of Silence

On 22nd May 2003, the Annual Intellectual Property Mock Trial took place in Oxford's Town Hall before a packed courtroom. The Honourable Justice Robin Jacob, senior judge of the Patents Court, held that one cannot copyright silence.

"The Mock Trial is an excellent occasion to see how a case involving a breach of intellectual property based on real facts would actually be conducted in a British court," said Professor David Vaver, Director of the OIPRC and organiser of the Mock Trial.

The barristers argued the case and cross-examined witnesses just as they would were they running the case in the Chancery Division of the High Court. Acting Counsel for the Claimant was Mr. Michael Silverleaf QC and for the Defendant was Mr. Henry Carr QC. The Claimant, Charles Hopin, was acted by Mr. Harry Small of Baker & McKenzie Solicitors and the Defendant Sally Airie by Ms. Anna Edwards-Stuart, a barrister in the Chambers of Mr. Silverleaf and Mr. Carr. Professor Vaver explains that the Mock Trial proceedings may be conducted seriously but not without humour, and never boringly—not only because of the quality of the participants but because of the nature of the case argued—some teasingly difficult area of the law.

The mock case dealt with the Claimant, Zen-inspired composer, Charles Hopin, suing the London-based band, The Electric Nun for allegedly copying Hopin's musical score '360 seconds' of silence in the Nuns' own musical work '90 and a bell'.

The facts of the mock case were based closely on last year's real dispute involving John Cage's Estate v Mike Batt. This case was settled out of court. In this case, Mike Batt, an arranger and songwriter, was challenged by the estate of John Cage for breach of copyright with regard to his track called 'A One Minute Silence' which he had included in his classical/rock fusion music album called 'Classical Graffiti'.

'A One Minute Silence' was said to comprise a reproduction of John Cage's piece called 4'33", which was first performed at a concert in Woodstock in 1952.

Mike Batt's album was very successful and within a few months of its reaching the top of the classical pop-chart, Cage's publishers, Peters Edition, made the claim against Mike Batt. After lengthy correspondence, Mike Batt made a settlement out of court with the representatives of the late John Cage and this amount of money is rumoured to be £100,000.

The intriguing question, a variant of which was the subject of the Mock Trial, was whether a work such as Cage's qualified for copyright as a musical work, and whether a rather different period of silence nevertheless could infringe any copyright. A side issue was also whether Cage could complain that he has been falsely attributed as the co-author of the CD's silent work.

Counsel for the Claimant relied on the case British Northrop Ltd v Texteam Blackburn Ltd [1976] R.P.C. 344. In this case, the Plaintiffs were granted an injunction to restrain the defendants from infringing the Plaintiffs' Copyright in a sales circular of specified simple drawings of spare parts such as screws and bolts by use of the trademark 'Northrop'. In the Mock Trial, the Claimant argued that the Defendant, in putting the Claimant's name as co-author on her work, had also infringed her copyright and his moral right not to have work misattributed to him.

Counsel for the Defendant relied on the 'Noah's Ark' dispute Plimer v Roberts and Another NG 480 of 1997, Federal Court of Australia, in which Professor Plimer Professor of Geology and Head of the School of Earth Sciences at the University of Melbourne, accused Dr. Roberts, a theologian, of plagiarism in an article about the disputed Noah's Ark site, a site of a boat-shaped formation which rests at 6,300 feet above sea-level in Eastern Turkey, about 12–15 miles from the summit of Greater Mount Arafat. It was alleged that Dr. Roberts used Professor Plimer's archaeological and scientific work, changing the findings to support the biblical account of Noah's Ark. The Defendants claimed their addition to Professor Plimer's work created a different work.

"Fascinating issues that raise questions of interest to lawyers, musicians, students and anyone interested in how justice is done in a British court in a civil case", explains Professor Vaver.

This Mock Trial was based on a true case reported in the UK newspapers on 28th September 2002. In the true story on which this Mock Trial was based, the songwriter and record producer Mike Batt was sued by the estate of the late composer John Cage. Mike Batt is a millionaire. Mike Batt was the man behind the success of the hit songs for the TV Series "THE WOMBLES OF WIMBLE-DON". He was accused of stealing the silence piece when, earlier in 2002 he included a self-explanatory track called A MINUTE OF SILENCE on his classical/fusion album CLASSICAL GRAFFITI. It seemed a deliberate but innocuous echo of 4'33", the four minutes and thirty three seconds of silence with which John Cage once outraged audiences, which was first performed in Woodstock in 1952.

The record CLASSICAL GRAFFITI soared to the top of the classical charts, where it remained for 3 months, but after two months John Cage's publishers, Peters Edition, contacted Mike Batt and sued him. It is rumoured that Mike Batt paid John Cage's estate £100,000 in an out-of-court settlement.

MATERIALS USED IN THE MOCK TRIAL—MUSIC OF SILENCE

1. Copyright, Designs and Patents Act 1988;

2. Extract of an article titled "Creationists v Scientists";

3. Professor Snelling's article about a massive boat-shaped formation on Mount Ararat;

4. Extract from the Institute for Creation Research on the global flood of Noah's day;

5. Extract from case report Plimer v Roberts

6. Extract from case report British Northrop v Texteam Blackburn Ltd [1976] RPC 344;

7. Extract from a report of the Woodstock performance of John Cage's 4'33".

1. **Copyright, Designs and Patents Act 1988**

CHAPTER 1

Subsistence, Ownership and Duration of Copyright.

Introductory

Copyright and copyright works

1(1) Copyright is a property right which subsists in accordance with this Part in the following descriptions of work—

    (a) original literary, dramatic, musical or artistic works,

    (b) sound recordings, films, broadcasts or cable programmes, and

    (c) the typographical arrangement of published editions.

(2) In this Part "copyright work" means a work of any of those descriptions in which copyright subsists.

(3) Copyright does not subsist in a work unless the requirements of this Part with respect to qualification for copyright protection are met (see section 153 and the provisions referred to there).

Rights subsisting in copyright works.

2(1) The owner of the copyright in a work of any description has the exclusive right to do the acts specified in Chapter II as the acts restricted by the copyright in a work of that description.

(2) In relation to certain descriptions of copyright work the following rights conferred by Chapter IV (moral rights) subsists in flavour of the author, director or commissioner of the work, whether or not he is the owner of the copyright—

    (a) section 77 (right to be identified as author or director),

    (b) section 80 (right to object to derogatory treatment of work), and

    (c) section 85 (right to privacy of certain photographs and films).

Literary, dramatic and musical works.

3(1) In this Part—

"literary work" means any work, other than a dramatic or musical work, which is written, spoken or sung, and accordingly includes

(a) a table or compilation [other than a data-base],

(b) a computer program,

(c) preparatory design material for a computer program, and

"dramatic work" includes a work of dance or mime; and

"musical work" means a work consisting of music, exclusive of any words or action intended to be sung, spoken or performed with the music.

(2) Copyright does not subsist in a literary, dramatic or musical work unless or until it is recorded, in writing or otherwise; and references in this Part to the time at which such a work is made are to the time at which it is so recorded.

(3) It is immaterial for the purposes of subsection(2) whether the work is recorded by or with the permission of the author; and where it is not recorded by the author, nothing in that subsection affects the question whether copyright subsists in the record as distinct from the work recorded.

Databases.

3A.(1). In this Part a literary work consisting of a database is original if, and only if, by reason of the selection or arrangement of the contents of the database the database constitutes the author's own intellectual creation.

Artistic works.

4(1) In this Part "artistic work" means

(a) a graphic work, photograph, sculpture or collage, irrespective of artistic quality,

(b) a work of architecture being a building or a model for a building, or

(c) a work of artistic craftsmanship.

(2) In the Part—

"building" includes any fixed structure, and a part of a building or fixed structure;

"graphic work" includes—

(a) any painting, drawing, diagram, map, chart or plan, and

(b) any engraving, etching, lithograph, woodcut or similar work;

"photograph" means a recording of light or other radiation on any medium on which an image is produced or from which an image may by any means be produced, and which is not part of a film;

"sculpure" includes a cast or model made for purposes of sculpture.

CHAPTER II

RIGHTS OF COPYRIGHT OWNER

The acts restricted by copyright.

The acts restricted by copyright in a work.

5(1) The owner of the copyright in a work has, in accordance with the following provisions of this Chapter, the exclusive right to do the following acts in the United Kingdom—

(a) copy the work (see section 17);

(b) to issue copies of the work to the public (see section 18);

(c) to perform, show or play the work in public;

(d) to broadcast the work or include it in a cable programme service;

(e) to make an adaptation of the work or do any of the above in relation to the adaptation;

and those acts are referred to in this Part as the "acts restricted by the copyright".

(2) Copyright in a work is infringed by a person who without the licence of the copyright owner does, or authorises another to do, any of the acts restricted by copyright.

(3) References of this Part to the doing of an Act restricted by copyright in a work are to the doing of it—

(a) in relation to the work as a whole or any substantial part of it, and

(b) either directly or indirectly;

and it is immaterial whether any intervening acts themselves infringe copyright.

(4) This Chapter has effect subject to—

(a) the provisions of Chapter III (acts permitted in relation to copyright works), and

(b) the provisions of Chapter VII)provisions with respect to copyright licensing).

Infringement of copyright by copying.

6(1) The copying of the work is an act restricted by the copyright in every description of copyright work; and references in this Part to copying and copies shall be construed as follows.

(2) Copying in relation to a literary, dramatic, musical or artistic work means reproducing the work in any material form. This includes storing the work in any medium or electronic means.

(3) In relation to an artistic work copying includes the making of a copy in three dimensions of a two-dimensional work and the making of a copy in two dimensions of a three-dimensional work.

(4) Copying in relation to a film, television broadcast or cable programme includes the making a photograph of the whole or any substantial part of any image forming part of the film, broadcast or cable programme.

(5) Copying in relation to any description of work includes the making of copies which are transient or are incidental to some other use of the work.

Infringement by issue of copies to the public.

7(1) The issue to the public of copies of the work is an act restricted by the copyright in every description of copyright work.

(2) References in this Part to the issue to the public of copies of a work do not include—

(a) any subsequent distribution, sale, hiring or loans of copies previously put into circulation (but see section 18A: infringement by rental or lending), or

(b) any subsequent importation of such copies into the United Kingdom or another EEA state,

except so far as paragraph (a) of subsection (2) applies to putting into circulation in the EEA copies previously put into circulation outside the EEA.

(3) References in this Part to the issue of copies of a work include the original issue of the original.

Adaptations.

8. An act which by virtue of this Chapter may be done without infringing copyright in a literary, dramatic or musical work does not, where that work is an adaptation, infringe any copyright in the work from which the adaptation was made.

CHAPTER IV

MORAL RIGHTS

Right to be identified as author or director.

9(1) The author of a copyright literary, dramatic, musical or artistic work, and the author of copyright film, has the right to be identified as the author or director of the work in the circumstances mentioned in this section; but the right is not infringed unless it has been asserted in accordance with section 78.

(2) The author of a literary work (other than words intended to be sung or spoken with music) or a dramatic work has the right to be identified whenever—

(a) the work is published commercially, performed in public, broadcast or included in a cable programme service, or

(b) copies of a film or sound recording including the work are issued to the public;

and that right includes the right to be identified whenever any of those events occur in relation to an adaptation of the work as the author of the work from which the adaptation was made.

(3) The author of a musical work, or a literary work consisting of words intended to be sung or spoken with music, has the right to be identified whenever—

(a) the work is published commercially;

(b) copies of a sound recording of the work are issued to the public; or

(c) a film of which the sound-track includes the work is shown in public or copies of such a film are issued to the public;

and that right includes the right to be identified whenever any of those events occur in relation to an adaptation of the work as the author of the work from which the adaptation was made.

(4) The author of an artistic work has the right to be identified whenever—

(a) the work is published commercially or exhibited in public, or a visual image of it is broadcast or included in a cable programme service;

(b) a film including a visual image of the work is shown in public or copies of such a film are issued to the public ; or

(c) in the case of a work of architecture in the form of a building or a model for a building, a sculpture or a work of artistic craftsmanship, copies of a graphic work representing it, or of a photograph of it, are issued to the public.

(5) The author of a work of architecture in the form of a building also has a right to be identified on the building as constructed or, where more than one building is constructed to the design, on the first to be constructed.

(6) The director of a film has the right to be identified whenever the film is shown in public, broadcast or included in a cable programme service or copies of the film are issued to the public.

(7) The right of the author or director under this section is—

(a) in the case of commercial publication or the issue to the public of copies of a film or sound recording, to be identified on each copy or, if that is not appropriate, in some other manner likely to bring his identity to the notice of the person acquiring a copy,

(b) in the case of identification on a building, to be identified by appropriate means visible to persons entering or approaching the building, and

(c) in any other case, to be identified in a manner likely to bring his identity to the attention of a person seeing or hearing the performance, exhibition, broadcast or cable programme in question;

and the identification must in each case be clear and reasonably prominent

(8) If the author or director in asserting his right to be identified specifies a pseudonym, initials or some other particular form of identification, that form shall be used; otherwise any reasonable form of identification may be used.

(9) This section has effect subject to section 79.

Requirement that right be asserted.

10(1) A person does not infringe the right conferred by section 77 by doing any of the acts mentioned in that section unless the right has been asserted in accordance with the following provisions so as to bind him in relation to that act.

(2) The right may be asserted generally, or ion relation to any specified act or description of Acts—

(a) on an assignment of copyright in the work, by including in the instrument effecting the assignment a statement that the author or director asserts in relation to that work his right to be identified, or

(b) by instrument in writing signed by the author or director.

(3) The right may also be asserted in relation to the public exhibition of an artistic work—

(a) by securing that when the author or other first owner of copyright parts with possession of the original, or of a copy made by him or under his direction or control, the author is identified on the original or copy, or on a frame, mount or other thing to which it is attached, or

(b) by including in a licence by which the author or other first owner of copyright authorises the making of copies of the work a statement signed by or on behalf of the person granting the licence that the author asserts his right to be identified in the event of the public exhibition of a copy made in pursuance of the licence.

(4) The persons bound by an assertion of the right under subsection (2) or (3) are—

(a) in the case of an assertion under subsection (2)(a), the assignee and anyone claiming through him, whether or not he has notice of the assertion;

(b) in the case of an assertion under subsection (2)(b), anyone to whose notice the assertion is brought;

(c) in the case of an assertion under subsection (3)(a), anyone into whose hands that original or copy comes, whether or not the identification is still present or visible;

(d) in the case of an assertion under subsection (3)(b), the licensee and anyone into whose hands a copy made in pursuance of the licence comes, whether or not he has notice of the assertion.

(5) In an action for infringement of the right the court shall, in considering remedies, take into account any delay in asserting the right.

Exceptions to right.

11(1) The right conferred by section 77 is subject to the following exceptions.

(2) The right does not apply in relation to the following descriptions of work—

(a) a computer program;

(b) the design of a typeface;

(c) any computer-generated work.

(3) The right does not apply to anything done by or with the authority of the copyright owner where copyright in the work originally vested—

(a) in the author's employer by virtue of section 11(2) (works produced in the course of employment), or

(b) in the director's employer by virtue of section 9(2)(a) (person to be treated as author of film).

2. **Extract of an article "creationists v scientists" 4.7.1997.**

There has been an on-going dispute between a Professor of sciences and a religious sects of fundamentalist Christians to do with Noah's Ark, mentioned in the Bible. Professor Ian Plimer was sued because he wrote a book called "Telling Lies for God", disclaiming Noah's Ark theory which was being put about by the Creationists.

3. **Professor Snelling's article about a massive boat-shaped formation on Mount Ararat.**

Mount Isa in Australia is one of the world's largest metal deposits with zinc and copper ore in the same beds. The zinc ore is found in thin layers of minerals alternating with bands of hardened mud. Most geologists today agree that the minerals at Mount Isa were originally deposited at the same time by underwater metal rich volcanic springs like those found at the Red Sea, Gulf of California and the East Pacific. Such a volcanic setting is reminiscent of the "fountains of the deep" during Noah's flood, and the fact that the shales which contain the metal ores are full of fossils, only reinforce this, Professor Snelling says.

But Professor Snelling refutes the claim that this verifies Noah's Ark. In 1948 an ariel photograph showed a boat-shape on top of Mount Ararat, the site being named as Durupinar site. Creationists claim that this is Noah's Ark from the Bible. The fact is that the "walls of the boat" are simply hardened mud containing boulders of the various local rock types and not petrified wood.

4. **Extract from the Institute for Creation Research on the Global Flood in Noah's day.**

Contrary to Proferror Snelling, the Institute for Creation Research state biblical arguments for a global flood of Noah's day. They say the following:

The depth and duration of the flood—the flood waters covered the mountains to a depth of at least the draft of Noah's Ark (Genesis 7:19,20).

The physical causes of the flood—the Bible explains that the breaking open of "all the fountains of the great deep" and the "windows of heaven" were the primary causes.(7:11).

The need for the Ark.

Destruction of all mankind.

Promise of no more floods.

The testimony of Jesus Christ (Luke 17:27).

The testimony of Peter (II Peter 3:10-12).

Many expressions of the flood's global nature (Genesis 41:57), (Genesis 7), (Genesis 8)(Genesis 9).

5. Extract from case-law report Plimer/Fasold v Roberts/Ark Search [1997]

This Australian case arose when a Professor Ian Plimer, Professor of geology at Melbourne University, a humanist, claimed that Roberts, a creationist, breached Professor's copyright and moral rights by using the Professor's material without permission and by making false and misleading statements in regard to Robert's promoted material sold as booklets and regarding an alleged "Ark site". Unlike Professor Snelling's findings that the site was a large block of bedrock uplifted by earthquake from which unstable mud flowing around the block has created the boat shape, partially covering the uplifted block, Professor Plimer asserted that the site was a syncline.

Professor Plimer then wrote a book "Telling lies for God" and changed his assertions that the site was a syncline to saying that the site is an allochthonous (transported) block and claimed this conclusion based on his own geological experience and he further suggested that Professor Snelling's work was plagiaristic.

Professor Plimer had previously been sued by Roberts for defamation and lost the case, paying substantial damages to Roberts.

David Fashold is a researcher whose material disproves the noah's Ark theory of the site on Mount Ararat. He claims with Plimer that Roberts used much of his material without permission. He and Plimer sued Roberts and the Ark Search, the Ark Search being composed of Christians who believe in the Bible and its account of the global flood.

The Court held that Dr Roberts did make misleading and deceptive statements in lectures he gave but that these were not commercial matters and that the subject of Noah's Ark is non-commercial in character. Although Dr Roberts was an author and had written about the Mount Ararat site, he was not carrying on a profession as author or speaker and he had received no payment for his lectures. It may be that Ark Search carried on a business, albeit an unsuccessful one, by selling tapes and videos to those who attended the lectures but that it was set up to assist Dr Roberts in progressing the search for Noah's Ark.

Plimer lost the case but appealed, where his appeal was dismissed. The Court of Appeal judge said:

"In giving his lectures, and contributing to the publications, Dr Roberts was not primarily motivated by a desire to promote any business activities of NARF. In giving his lectures, and contributing to the publications, Dr Roberts was not primarily motivated by a desire to promote any business activities of Noah's Ark Research Foundation. In his lectures, Dr Roberts spoke on the historic and relifgious significance of the site. The audience attending his lectures and the purchasers of the tapes and videos obtained that which they wished to hear, Dr Roberts' address on Noah's Ark and Mount Ararat. The relevant context in which the misleading statements were made was, in my opinion, not a business, trading or commercial one. The misleading statements were not "made in the course of, or for the purposes of, some trading or commercial dealing" between Dr Roberts and the members of the audience or the purchasers of the tapes and videos. The crucial distinction between "the central conception of trade and commerce" and the other activities is this…The position might well be different if the misleading statement was made in the course of, or for the purposes of, some trading or commercial dealing between the corporation and the particular employee. In this case there was no trading or commercial dealing or relationship between Dr Roberts and the members of his audience or the purchasers of the tapes and videos of his lectures….The appeal should be dismissed."

6. **Extract from the case report British Northrop v Texteam Blackburn Ltd [1976] RPC 344**

This is a copyright case in which interlocutory injunctions were granted to restrain infringement of copyright and trade mark. The plaintiff had copyright in the plaintiff's existing drawings. The defendants infringed that copyright by manufacturing machinery parts

7. **Extract from a report of the Woodstock performance of John Cage's 4'33".**

"The first performance of John Cage's 4'33" created a scandal. Written in 1952, it is Cage's most notorious composition, his so-called "silent piece". The piece consists of four minutes and thitry three seconds in which the performer plays nothing. At the premiere some listeners were unaware that they had heard nothing at all. It was first performed by the young pianist David Tudor at Woodstock, New York, on August 29,1952, for an audience supporting the Benefits Artists Welfare Fund—an audience that supported contemporary art.

Tudor placed the hand-written score, which was in conventional notation with blank measures, on the piano and sat motionless as he used a stopwatch to measure the time of each movement. The score indicated three silent movements, each of a different length, but when added together totalled four minutes and thirty three seconds. Tudor signalled its commencement by lowering the keyboard lid of the piano. The sound of the wind in the trees entered the first movement. It was then lowered for the second movement during which raindrops pattered on the roof. The score was in several pages, so he turned the pages as time passed, yet playing noting at all. The keyboard lid was raised and lowered again for the final movement, during which the audience whispered and muttered.

Cage said, 'People began whispering to one another, and some people began to walk out. They didn't laugh—they were just irritated when they realised nothing was going to happen, and they haven't forgotten it 30 years later: they're still angry'. Maverick Concert Hall, the site of the first performance, was ideal in allowing the sounds of the environment to enter, because the back of the hall was open to the surrounding forest. When Tudor finished, raising the keyboard lid and himself from the pianio, the audience first burst into an uproar—"infuriated and dismayed", according to the reports. Even in the midst of an avant garde concert attended by modern artists, 4'33" was considered "going too far"....."

INTRODUCTORY INTTELLECTUAL PROPERTY QUESTIONS

Question 1.

What are the principle objectives of Intellectual Property Law? Discuss commentators' views on the extent to which the law achieves its objectives?

Answer:

Intellectual Property law regulates the creation, use and exploitation of mental or creative labour.

Article 2, paragraph viii, WIPO Convention (1967) states that IP includes "the rights relating to—literary, artistic and scientific works—performances and performing artists, photographs and broadcasts—inventions in all fields of human endeavour—scientific discoveries—industrial designs, trade marks, service marks and commercial names and designations—protection against unfair competition and all other rights resulting from intellectual activity in the industrial, scientific, literary or artistic fields."

IP law protects application of ideas and information that are of commercial value. The law achieves its objectives by being negative rights, ie. rights to stop others doing certain things, eg. to stop pirates, counterfeiters, imitators, third parties who independently reached the same ideas, from exploiting them without the licence of the right-owner. IP law also achieves its objectives in a positive way, eg. the right to be granted a patent or register a trade-mark upon fulfilling the requisite conditions.

But Cornish says that "the right-owner does not need the right in order to exploit a market for its goods and services: a patent is not a pre-condition to exploiting one's own invention. The right gives no liberty to ignore the rights of other individuals or to over-ride public liability."

Bentley & Sherman say that (pg3) IP law is highly politicised and that right-holders have tended to argue that the existing laws provide inadequate protection, eg. the threshold for patent protection needs to be explicitly extended to cover software, that trade marks owners are not sufficiently protected against cyber squatters who acquire related domain names.

But in Mr.Justice Laddie's 1996 article[158], he says that copyright law "provides an over-abundance of protection to the monopoly right owner."

In the 1988 Copyright Act, the term of monopoly is specified as life of the author plus 50 years for literary, dramatic and musical works and a flat 50 years for computer-generated works, films, records and broadcasts. However, as a result of EC Term Directive, the copyright in literary works is now life of the author plus 70 full years. This additional 20 years has been imposed throughout the EU. The justification for this CANNOT be based on the principle of encouraging artistic creativity.

Question 2.

"One reason that Intellectual Property law may fail to achieve its objectives is that these objectives are incompatible. Identify some potential areas of conflict and consider whether it can ever be possible to resolve such conflicts."

Answer:

(a) IP law recognises the inherent value of individual creativity.

(b) IP law also recognises the economic and social benefits which are designed to flow from market protection.

These two objectives can be in conflict.

(a) tends towards universality, eg. the French d'roit d'auteur, which offered protection to authors of the world without distinction of nationality, even in advance of bilateral or multi-national relations with other countries.[159]

(b) sees no reason to give rights to foreigners whose own law does not provide equivalent benefit in return.

The objective (a) is reflected in the UK's Copyright Designs and Patents Act 1988.

Another area of conflict is the question of "damages against the innocent infringer".[160]

---

158 "Copyright: over-strength, over-regulated and over-rated? " (1996) EIPR
159 Cornish (1988) "article "The canker of reciprocity" EIPR
160 Roshana Kelbrick (1994) EIPR 204

Countries do not all share the English common law background. Australian and Canadian legal systems, unlike South Africa, do. But no court in either of these jurisdictions has held that an INNOCENT defendant is liable for damages in respect of trade mark infringement or passing off, and dicta by the courts seem to indicate that they would be loathe to reach such a decision. In South Africa, damages will not be awarded unless a defendant acts intentionally or negligently. Therefore, COMPLETE INNOCENCE on the part of a defendant will protect him against an award of damages in both trade mark and passing off proceedings.

In the common law tradition, copyright's principal purpose is considered to be its incentive function. Societies seek to encourage creativity by regarding it with property rights. There is the conflict of whether DATA, the key building blocks for creative endeavour, ought to become property. There is the internet and the position of on-line service providers and the question of massive copyright infringement it facilitates. There is the issue of determining which nation's laws ought to govern internet copyright infringement now that copyright materials may be made to flow across domestic borders at the click of a mouse.[161]

Question 3.

"In relation to international intellectual property agreements, what kinds of interests come into conflict, and why?"

Answer:

International IP agreements protect different nation's IP rights. The principle of national treatment allows countries the autonomy to develop and enforce their own laws, while meeting the demands for international protection.

eg. The Paris Convention for the Protection of Industrial Property 1883.

eg. The Berne Convention for the Protection of Literary and Artistic Works 1886.

The principle of national treatment provides rights owners with some protection in other jurisdictions.

---

161 Rickett, C.E.F & Austin, G.W, 2000, "International IP and the Common Law World", Harrt Publication.

One conflict is THE RIGHT OF PROTECTION and THE COST OF SUCH VAST PROTECTION. But this is now countered by an "international registration" which would take effect almost automatically in designated countries.

In 1994 there came into effect the TRIPs Agreement (WTO) which covers all areas of IP. It requires members of the WTO to recognise the existing standards of protection within the Berne and Paris Conventions.(Article 2(1) and Article 9). It contains detailed provisions on enforcement of IP rights which had before this been left to national law.

There is the 1996 WIPO Copyright Treaty which is yet to come into force.

One set of interests that come into conflict is due to the legal categories involved. Legal categories do not necessarily correspond to objects commonly associated with copyright law, eg. a book might contain a literary work, an artistic work and a typographical arrangement.

The case of _Electronic Technique v Critchley_[162] resulted in a refusal in summary judgement in circuit diagram copyright action as trial was required to determine whether defendant's behaviour amounted to substantial taking of plaintiff's copyright work over issue of flagrancy damages.

The EC Duration and Rental Directives require directors to be recognised as authors. It distinguishes between cinematographic works and related rights in mere fixations, so-called "films" or "video-games".

BUT exceptions to copyright protection available in the UK have been largely unaffected by regional or international influences. Under the Berne Convention, members of the EU are permitted to create exceptions to the exclusive rights in limited circumstances.

Exceptions to the reproduction right must satisfy the "3-step test". (Berne Convention, Article 9(2); TRIPs Agreement Article 13).

TRIPs requires ALL limitations to comply with the "3-step test".

Question 4.

"Explain the significance of Intellectual Property Law for Indigenous peoples. Is this an appropriate vehicle for achieving their objectives?"

---

162 Electronic Technique v Critchley [1997] FSR 401.

Answer:

With the exception of trivial or immoral information, no restrictions are placed on the subject matter that is protected by breach of confidence. So the action of breach of confidence can be used and has been used on, for example, the cultural and religious secrets of an Aboriginal Community.

In the case of Foster and others v Mountford and Rigby Ltd in the Supreme Court of the Northern Territory at alice Springs, the plaintiffs were members of an Aboriginal Council, the Pitjantjara Council and sought to restrain Mountford, an antropologist and writer and his publishers from publishing a book containing matter of deep religious and cultural significance to the Pitjanjara people which had been revealed to Mountford many years before. The plaintiffs gave evidence to the effect that much of what had been revealed was known only to the Pitjantjara people, some of it indeed only to the male portion of that people and that this matter had been so revealed in confidence. A further question arose as to whether the plaintiffs were entitled to sue as members of the Council rather than by a relator action. The relief sought was granted. It was held that what had been revealed to Mountford had been of a confidential character and had been revealed under a situation which imported an obligation of confidence.

Information is protected irrespective of the format in which it appears. The action applies equally to information when embodied in writing, drawings, photographs, goods or products or where it has been disclosed orally. The information does not need to be fixed or in a permanent form. As such, the information may be written, oral, encrypted, embodied in physical objects (whether it be the genetic code of a tree or the design of a product), or take shape as a formulae, a plan or a sketch.

BUT there are FOUR limitations placed on the type of information that may be protected under "breach of confidence":

- information that is trivial

- information that is immoral

- information that is vague or

- in the public domain.

In Australia[163], the National Indigenous Arts Advocy association recently estimated that the Aboriginal and Torres Strait Islander arts and culture industry generates around $200 million dollars a year. This is good reason for protecting their IP rights, especially against passing-off. Australia plans to introduce "labels of authenticity" and a "collaboration mark" which will be registered as certification marks. These indicate to the public that, irrespective of their trade source, the certified goods or services possess a specific quality or characteristic. The issue arises of whether the certifier is COMPETENT to certify goods or services and this depends on the certifier's ability to monitor and control approved users of the mark, augmented where necessary by inspection and sampling to ensure compliance. Training of certifiers is required but training programmes will require resources that may not be readily available. A percentage of the applicant's fees paid for use of the labels may set-off such a programme.

The COST OF TRAINING will have to be borne and burdens may be placed on regional and local organisations undertaking the certification process.

Another issue is the DEFINITION OF AUTHENTICITY. Indigenous artists need to comply with customary law. Under customary laws, rights to reproduce pre-existing designs is vested in the traditional custodians, depending on descent, kinship and marriage.

The recent decision in *Bulun Bulun v R & T Textiles Pty Ltd*. reinforces the importance of the relationship between the indigenous artist and their community and is justification for legal protection of indigenous peoples' rights in traditional artworks focusing on concepts of cultural integrity and individual community rights in Aboriginal traditional designs. The case involved an action for copyright infringement relating to a painting "Magpie Geese and Water Lilies at the Waterhole" created by Johnny Bulun Bulun. As well as finding that Bulun Bulun's copyright had been infringed, the Federal Court of Australia also held that Bulun Bulun owed his community a fiduciary duty in relation to the stories depicted in the painting. This was because of the "trust and confidence" that arose when Bulun Bulun was given permission to use the Community's traditional ritual knowledge in the painting. Had Bulun Bulun not taken action to protect the knowledge, the court suggested that because of the fiduciary relationship that existed between Bulun Bulun and his community, the elders of the community might have stood in his place and brought the action.

---

163 Leanne Wiseman's article "Protection of Indigenous Art & Culture in Australia: The Labels of Authenticity" EIPR 2001.

It is to be noted that there is at present no intention to register the "labels of authenticity" as certification marks outside Australia. So there is the real possibility of foreign goods and services CLAIMING TO BE INDIGENOUS being imported INTO Australia.

It is argued[164] that IP rules entrench the advantages/disadvantages position of some to the detriment of others as far as BIOLOGICAL RESOURCES are concerned. It is argued that rich nations have AN UNFAIR BARGAINING ADVANTAGE. They provide development aid to poor nations, lead and significantly influence policy in international development organisations, ensuring protection of their interests.

Referring knowledge held by others as "informal, indigenous, traditional or local" paints this knowledge with inferior connotations. Traditional communities such as those found in Africe did not keep their knowledge documented in written form and such knowledge is downgraded to "informal knowledge".

Question 5.

"Compare the roles of WIPO and WTO in the international management of intellectual property rights".

Answer:

WIPO has 50 years of experience in IP on a global scale. It administers the Paris and Berne Conventions. WIPO is a sub-division of the United Nations and is responsible the Berne and Paris Conventions and also oversees a number of specialised treaties, such as those that protect semi-conductor chip designs and sound recordings. WIPO hosts meetings at which national delegations discuss possible revisions of existing treaties and proposals for new treaties. WIPO will convene a diplomatic conference to consider draft treaties, eg. in 1996, a conference to consider supplements to the Berne Convention to extend the rights on performers and producers of sound recordings and a conference to consider a new treaty to protect the contents of databases. It is to be noted that the US did not join the Berne Union until 1989.

---

164 Morris Mudiwa's article "Indigenous knowledge and IP rights: biodiversity resource rich, economically poor communities versus biodiversity resource poor, economically rich nations" 2002.

The WTO has an annex, the TRIPs Agreement of 1994. It is to be noted that the US was central in concluding the TRIPs Agreement.

The TRIPs Agreement was adopted in part because of dissatisfaction with WIPO processes. TRIPs persuades countries to comply **voluntarily** with the letter and spirit of TRIPs norms.

TRIPs establishes minimum protection standards not just for copyright, but also rights in sound recordings and broadcasts, trade marks, industrial designs, patents, semi-conductor chip designs and trade secrets by incorporating provisions of Berne and Paris Conventions but it does so selectively.

The **moral rights provision** of the Berne Convention **is OMITTED in TRIPs.**

The Unfair Competition provision of the Paris Convention is incorporated in TRIPs but only in so far as it provides a framework for protection of undisclosed information (ie. trade secrets).

Also, TRIPs establishes some norms NOT found in the major conventions, eg requiring WTO members to regulate the rental sound recordings, computer programs and motion pictures.

Also, TRIPs, like WIPO, obliges countries to respect national treatment principles.

TRIPs has a dispute settlement process—an international mechanism with which to resolve complaints about inadequacies of IP protection. A State can file a complaint with the WTO alleging a violation of TRIPs. If efforts at conciliation and mediation are unsuccessful, TRIPs will convene a panel of experts on the validity of the complaint. If the panel upholds the complaint, the offending nation has to either adjust its laws or face trade sanctions by the victor. Trade sanctions may be levied against products unrelated to the violation of TRIPs norms.

TRIPs Council oversees national policy making and judicial enforcement.

Question 6

"The first WTO decision on TRIPs in 1997 concerned India's approach to pharmaceutical patents. Explain the issues raised by the case and evaluate the WTO approach to these issues.

Answer:

A few hours before the commencement of the WTO, the President of India promulgated an Ordinance amending the Indian Patents Act 1970 expressly bringing it into line with TRIPs patent standards.

The Act now provides the product patents in the fields of agricultural chemicals and pharmaceuticals.

Exclusive marketing rights are granted to overseas patentees and compulsory licensing is permitted where the exercise of exclusive marketing rights by a grantee "does not meet the reasonable requirements of the public, or the product concerned is not available to the public at a reasonable price."

Under Article 70.8 and 70.9 of the TRIPs Agreement, India was required to provide a means of receipt of applications for product patents for pharmaceuticals and agricultural chemicals and to grant exclusive marketing rights on fulfilment of certain conditions.

It was the US which pressured for this.

Since then, India established a mailbox system through administrative instructions.[165]

More than 2,200 applications have been filed by US companies. No exclusive marketing rights (EMR) applications have so far been filed.

In respect of Article 70.8, the dispute raised by the US related only to the legal security of the patents applications filed in the mailbox system established through administrative instructions.

Question 7.

"Examine the significance of the TRIPs Agreement, particularly in relation to enforcement."

Answer:

The TRIPs Agreement enshrined detailed rules on the enforcement of IP rights.

---

165 www.indianembassy.org

The TRIPs Agreement sought to stem the flaws of the WIPO which administered the Berne and Paris Conventions.

The perceived flaws were:

1. The absence of detailed rules on the enforcement of rights before national judicial administrative authorities, and

2. The absence of a binding and effective dispute—settlement mechanism for disputes between States.

The TRIPs Agreement requires that members comply with the substantive provisions of the Paris and Berne Conventions.

Articles 2(1)[166] and 9(1)[167] have the effect of imposing the obligations contained in those provisions to countries not party to the Conventions, while integrating all WTO members in the TRIPS framework, notably as regards dispute settlement.

The TRIPS provisions were drafted so as to create a positive obligation to comply, ie, to take the necessary steps to bring national legislation in line with the relevant provisions of the Paris Convention. TRIPS is a Paris-plus and Berne-plus agreement.

Articles 3 and 4 guarantee national treatment (treatment of foreign rightholders no less favourable than treatment of nationals) and the most-favoured-nation treatment, where benefits accorded nationals of a specific country must be extended to nationals of other Contracting States.).

Article 6 excludes from the dispute settlement the question of "exhaustion of rights", otherwise known as "parallel importation", ie. the importation of

---

166 TRIPS Agreement, article 2(1)

"In respect of Parts II, III and IV of this Agreement, Members shall comply with Articles 1 through 12, and Article 19, of the Paris Convention(1967).

167 TRIPS Agreement, article 9(1)

"Members shall comply with Articles 1 through 21 of the Berne Convention (1971) and the Appendix thereto. However, Members shall not have rights or obligations under this Agreement in respect of the rights conferred under Article 6 bis of that Convention or of the rights derived therefrom."

goods lawfully manufactured in another country and generally intended for distribution in that country.

Article 10 [168] of TRIPS is the first provision in any multilateral instrument to confirm the protection of computer programs by copyright. As regards databases and other "compilations", Article 10(2) confirms the application of copyright to databases.

Article 11[169] establishes a rental right on computer programs and films.

Article 14(4)[170] establishes a rental right on sound recordings.

---

168 TRIPS Agreement, Article 10:

"1. Computer programs, whether in source or object code, shall be protected as literary works under the Berne Convention(1971).

2.Compilations of data or other material, whether in machine readable or other form, which by reason of the selection or arrangement of their contents constitute intellectual creations shall be ptotected as such. Such protection, which shall not extend to the data or material itself, shall be without prejudice to any copyright subsisting in the data or material itself."

169 TRIPS Agreement, Article 11:

"In respect of at least computer programs and cinematographic works, a Member shall provide authors and their successors in title the right to authorise or to prohibit the commercial rental to the public of originals or copies of their copyright works. A Member shall be excepted from this obligation in respect of cinematographic works unless such rental has led to widespread copying of such works which is materially impairing the exclusive right of reproduction conferred in that Member on authors and their successors in title. In respect of computer programs, this obligation does not apply to rentals where the program itself is not the essential object of the rental."

170 TRIPS Agreement, Article 14(4):

"The provisions of Article 11 in respect of computer programs shall apply mutatis mutandis to producers of phonograms and any other right holders in phonograms as determined in a Member's law. If on 15 April 1994 a Member has in force a system of equitable remuneration of right holders in respect of the rental of phonograms, it may maintain such system provided that the commercial rental of phonograms is not giving rise to the material impairment of the exclusive rights of reproduction of right holders."

Article 15(1)[171]defines the expression "trade mark". This definition is very broad and does not limit the types of signs that may be considered a trade mark and it includes service marks.

ENFORCEMENT

Before TRIPS, provisions dealing with enforcement of rights were basically general obligations to provide for legal remedies and, in certain cases, seizure of infringing goods. It was otherwise left to national legislation.

Article 42 provides for the existence of civil judicial proceedings covering all the rights protected under the TRIPS Agreement. It includes a prohibition of overly burdensome requirements concerning mandatory personal appearances.

The Article also guarantees the right to present all relevant evidence to substantiate one's claims.

Article 44 makes injunctions available "in order to desist from an infringement, inter alia, to prevent the entry into the channels of commerce in their jurisdiction of imported goods that involve the infringement of an intellectual property right."

Article 46 provides that judicial authorities must have been the authority to order that seized goods be disposed of outside the channels of commerce. Article 46 addresses the question of certain counterfeit goods to which an infringing mark is affixed.

Article 50 provides for inaudita altera parte (ex parte) action, which is often the only effective means of combating piracy and counterfeiting.

---

171 TRIPS Agreement, Article 15(1):
"Any sign, or any combination of signs, capable of distinguishing the goods or services of one undertaking from those of other undertakings, shall be capable of constituting a trademark. Such signs, in particular words including personal names, letters, numerals, figurative elements and combinations of colours as well as any combination of such signs, shall be eligible for registration as trademarks. Where signs are not inherently capable of distinguishing the relevant goods or services, Members may make registrability depend on distinctiveness acquired through use. Members may require, as a condition of registration, that signs be visually perceptible."

Quick and effective measures are ordered.

Preventive injunctions must be available in respect of "qualified acts".

Article 51 adds border measures. In pirated copyright and counterfeit trade marked goods, a procedure must be made available before a "competent" authority to a right-holder to lodge an application for suspension of the release of goods. No such procedures has existed before.

Article 61 provides for criminal measures, often considered essential in the fight against infringement.

Question 8.

"What does counterfeiting mean, and what problems does it cause? Why is it necessary to achieve international agreement in tackling these problems?

Answer:

Piracy and counterfeiting is a major trade in many parts of the world. The music, film, computer, pharmaceutical and luxury goods trades have had to set up joint organisations to combat infringement on a commercial scale.

The Regulation laying down measures to prohibit the release for free circulation, export or transit of counterfeit and pirated goods (COM(93)329 final) [1993]O.J.238/15

1.2. "for the purposes of this Regulation:

    (a) "Counterfeit goods" means:

- goods, including the packaging, thereof, bearing without authorisation, a trademark which is identical to the trademark validly registered in respect of the same type of goods, or which cannot be distinguished in its essential aspects from such trademark, and which thereby infringes the rights of the owner of the trademark in question under Community Law of the Member State where the application for action by the customs authorities is made,

- any trademark symbol (logo), whether or not presented separately, in the same circumstances as the goods referred to in the first indent;

- any tool, mould or similar material specifically intended for the manufacture of a counterfeit trademark or of a product bearing such a trademark, provided such tools, moulds or materials infringe community law or the law of the Member State where the application for action by the customs authorities is made;

- packaging materials bearing the trade marks of counterfeiting products, presented separately, in the same circumstances as the goods referred to in the first indent;"

The TRIPS Agreement calls for enforcement procedure which permit effective action against IP infringement, "including expeditious remedies to prevent infringements and remedies which constitute a deterrent to further infringement" (Article 41). At the same time the measures must avoid being barriers to legitimate trade and provide safeguards against abuse.

Under TRIPS, civil process must be provided which may lead to injunctive as well as compulsory relief and delivery up for destruction of infringing material and means of producing it.

It is mandatory to have provisional procedures for preventing infringement of IP rights and preserving relevant evidence. Against the importation of counterfeit trade mark goods and pirated copyright goods there must be arrangements for customs seizure. The activities must be treated as serious criminal offences with accompanying measures for seizure, forfeiture and destruction.

In many situations, counterfeit products originate from other jurisdictions. There are 2 legal mechanisms for stopping articles that infringe IP rights entering the UK. The EU's Infringing Goods Regulation is one set of procedures and domestic legislation is another. Goods which infringe IP rights can be retained by customs authorities when they are introduced to or exported from the Community.

Question 9.

On the basis of previous case law, how are the courts likely to interpret the term "distinctive" for the purpose of trademark registration?

Answer:

The trade Marks Act 1994 defines a trademark as "any sign capable of being represented graphically which is capable of distinguishing the goods or services of a particular trader from those of other undertakings".

Under this definition, 3-D shapes, sounds (and possibly smells) if capable of being presented graphically, are now registrable.

This new Act places a greater duty of care and responsibility on trademark owners.

The 1994 Act expands the definition of trademark infringement established under the Trade Marks Act 1938.

The DTI describes the PURPOSE of a trade mark as to "assert and define the origin of goods, and protect the reputation of their producer and their investment in advertising and promoting brand".

The UK Trade Marks Act 1994 is based on the EEC Council Directive 89/104.

The UK adheres to all main conventions governing IP.

The Paris Convention on Industrial Property.

The Berne Convention for the Protection of Literary and Artistic Works.

The European Patent Convention.

The Rome Convention on the Protection of Performers, producers of Phonograms and Broadcasting Organisations.

The Protocol of the Madrid Agreement on Trade Mark registration.

The Patent Co-operation Treaty.

The UK is also a member of the Agreement on Trade Related Aspects of IP Rights (TRIPS Agreement) which formed part of the GATT Uruguay Round concluded at 15th December 1993 and signed 15th April 1994. All States which subscribe to the WTO become bound to a mutual recognition of IP rights at a high level of protection.

In the 1913 case *Registrar of Trade Marks v W & G DuCRos Ltd* motor cab proprietors in London applied for registration as trade marks for motor vehicles of two marks used by them for 3 years and in connection with their motor cabs in London. One mark consisted of the letters "W & G" written in a running hand with a distorted tail to the G ending up under the W.

The other mark consisted of "W & G" in ordinary block letters.

These marks had in fact become "distinctive" in the London district but not elsewhere.

It was held that the marks were NOT distinctive within the meaning of s9(5) Trade Marks Act 1905 and were therefore not registrable.

In the recent case of <u>BP Amoco plc v John Kelly Ltd [2001]</u> the issue was whether the defendant;s use of colour green on service stations in Northern Ireland was infringement of BP's registered colour marks under section 10 of the 1994 Act and of passing off. BP had applied in 1991 under the Trade Marks Act 1938 for the registration of two colour marks: first, in respect of oils and greases, etc. all within class 4 and secondly, in respect of vehicle washes, service stations, vehicle maintenance in class 37.

The class 4 application stated that "the mark consists of the colour green applied to the exterior surfaces of the premises used for the supply of the said goods as depicted in the representation (photo) attached".

The class 37 application for a registered service mark was in virtually identical terms.

The Court held that the colour registrations were valid but NOT infringed and rejected the claim in passing off.

In the case of *Philips Electronics v Remington [1998]* the criteria for registrability of trade mark of SHAPE of goods or packaging was the issue. The validity of registration of pictorial trade mark of the 3-headed rotary shaver was challenged. The Phillips trade mark was held INVALID and not infringed.

The case concerned the Phillips 3-headed rotary shaver, a design which Philips made since 1966. They are sold under and marked with the mark Philishave. Then Remington introduced its 3-headed rotary shaver into England and Philips sued for infringement of its relevant pictorial trade mark registration. Philips claimed to assert its shaver mark as a famous mark under Article 6 bis of the Paris Convention, implemented by section 56 Trade Marks Act 1994.

Philips relied on "DISTINCTIVENESS" acquired through advertising, and on the evidence of trade witnesses and members of the public. The evidence was directed to the distinctiveness of their shavers as a whole, rather than of the shaver mark as such.

Justice Jacobs held that any distinction between the shaver mark anf the real 3-d object was irrelevant. As to what was distinctive about the shavers, the judge placed weight on the fact that they were always marked "Philishave".

Question 10.

What is meant by "graphical representation" for the purpose of trade mark registration? Are there any potential problems with this requirement?

Answer:

The Trade Marks Act 1994, in force since 31st October 1994, and implementing the EC Directive Harmonisation of Trade Mark Law defines a trademark as "any sign capable of being REPRESENTED GRAPHICALLY which is capable of distinguishing goods and services of one undertaking from those of other undertakings". Under this definition, 3-D shapes, sounds (and possibly smells) if capable of being represented graphically, are now registrable.

So one hurdle that must be met for a trade mark to be validly registered under s1(1) Article 4, is that the sign must be "capable of capable of being represented graphically".

The sign must be "capable of distinguishing the goods or services of one undertaking from the goods or services of another" [Article 4 s 1(1)].

S1(1) thus excludes from registration signs that do not have the feature of a trade mark (*Philips Electronic v Remington [1999]*).

The provisions help to ensure that trade marks function to guarantee to the consumer or end-user the identity or origin of the product to which it is applied (*Bach Flower Remedies v Healing Herbs[2000]*).

The problems raised will be because of s3(1)(a) which provides that failure to comply with any of the requirements of s1(1) is one of the ABSOLUTE grounds which a sign will NOT be registered.

In the case *AD2000 Trade Mark [1997] RPC 168* it was held to mean no more than "not incapable" of distinguishing the applicant's goods from those of others.

The uncertainty that surrounds the relationship between s1(1) and s3(1)(a) and s3(1)(b) appear self-contradictory.

S1(1) provides that an applicant may only register a sign that is capable of distinguishing the goods or services of one undertaking from those of others and s3(1)(b) provides that a sign may be refused protection on the basis that it is "deviod of distinctive character".

So if a mark is non-registerable by virtue of s3(1)(b)—(d), it is still possible for the mark to be registered because s(3) states that a trade mark shall not be refused registration under s3(1)(b)—(d) if the trade mark has IN FACT acquired a distinctive character as a result of the use made of it ie, where a mark may be inherently non-registerable, it is possible for it to become registerable through USE.In the case of *Bach Flower Remedies v Healing Herbs* the Court of Appeal has rejected the idea that the test of capacity to distinguish must be applied in a manner which treats the meaning of signs as forever set in stone. The case concerned whether the words BACH FLOWER REMEDIES were capable of DISTINGUISHING the homoeopathic procucts marketed by the claimant, given that other products on the market employed the teachings og Edward Bach. At first instance the mark had been held to be DESCRIPTIVE and on appeal it was sought to overturn that finding in the light of evidence OF USE. The Court of appeal said it was first necessary to see if the mark had "capacity to distinguish". It was held that it had no "capacity to distinguish".

So, in certain circumstances, a word can become used in such a way that it is inconceivable that, without further addition, it will ever be able to acquire distinctiveness. Bach Flower Remedies has become as inseparably linked with a product as "soap" had with soap.

But, the UK Registry Work Manual explains that a sign is graphically represented when (*Antoni & Alison's Application/Vacuum Packing [1998] OJ OHIM 3/180*) it is possible to determine from the graphical representation precisely what the sign is that the applicant uses without the need for supporting samples, etc; the graphical representation can stand in the place of the sign used or proposed to be used by the applicant because it represents that sign and no other; and it is reasonably practicable for persons inspecting the register, or reading the Trade Marks Journal, to understand from the graphical representation what the trade mark is. (TMR Work Manual, chapter 6, para 2.3)

The problems that arise where an applicant simply relies upon words to represent more unusual marks can be seen in *Swizzels Matlow's Trade Mark Application [1998] RPC 244*, where an application to register a shape mark was rejected. In the application the description of the mark read "the trade mark consists of a chewy sweet on a stick for non-medicated confectionery". The TMR rejected the application, primarily on the basis that it was neither possible nor practicable for anyone inspecting the register to determine what the trade mark was from the description. The words "chewy" and "sweets" and "sticks" could be interpreted very widely and, in combination, covered 'an infinite variety' and would need the benefit of supporting material, namely, samples of the goods.

ONE POTENTIAL PROBLEM AREA is colour marks. The colours brown or red, eg, cannot be registered because they are too vague to form a graphical representation of the sign. (TMR Work Manual)

In the case *Orange Personal Communications Services/Orange R 7/97-3 [1998] OJ OHIM 5/040*, an application which simply stated in words that the mark comprised the colour "orange" was refused because such a representation was too imprecise, since innumerable colour shades would fall under such a broad generic term. Also, a scientific description such as ;a blue bottle of optical characteristics such that if the wall thickness of 3 mm the bottle has, in air, a dominant wavelength of 472–474 nonometres, a purity of 44–48%, an optical brightness of 28–32%' is INADEQUATE because it does not give immediate and unambiguous idea of what the mark is. (*Ty Nant Spring Water [1999] RPC 55,59.*)

Question 11.

What do the cases of *Philips v Remington* and *Re Dualit Ltd* tell us about the English courts' approach to registration of the SHAPE of goods?

Answer:

In the case *Philips Electronics v Remington [1998]* the criteria for registerability of trade mark of shape of goods or packaging was the issue.

S3(2)(a)/Article 7(1)(e)(I) CTMR provide that a sign shall not be registered where it consists exclusively of a shape which results from the nature of the goods themselves. The qusetion of what is meant by "the goods themselves" was considered in Philips v Remington where the issue was whether the shape of a 3-headed rotary shaver fell within the scope of s3(2)(a).

It was agreed that the goods were electrical shavers and that the goods refer to the goods in respect of which the trade is registered.

In this case, the shape of the razor did NOT fall foul of s3(2)(a) because there were a number of shapes other than the one in question that a 3-headed electric shaver could have taken. THEREFORE, the shape did not result from the nature of the goods themselves. So if the applicant can demonstrate that there are other shapes of the same goods on the market, no objection under s3(2)(a) will be sustainable.

In *Re Dualit [1999] RPC 890*, Justice Lloyd held that an application which related to the shape of a toaster lacked distinctive character: there was nothing about the shape alone which, apart from evidence of USE, makes it inherently distinctive as a badge of origin of the applicant's products. The relevant class of persons is not trade buyers but the average customer of the product. (*Re Dualit*, pp 890,898. para 33)

Question 12. Explain the meaning of "comparative advertising" and illustrate how the courts' interpretation of Trade Marks Act 1994 s10(6) has changed the legal framework for this activity.

Answer:

The rules relating to Comparative Advertising were amended in April 2000 with the implementation of Directive 97/55/EC relating to the Control of Misleading Advertising.

The amending legislation was enacted in the form of the Control of Misleading Advertisements (Amendment) Regulation 2000 which expressly includes reference to comparative advertising.

S10(6) TMA 1994 allows the use of a competitor's registered trade mark, provided the use is for the purpose of identifying goods or services as those of the proprietor or a licensee. But any other use otherwise than in accordance with honest practices in industrial or commercial matters shall be treated as infringing the registered trade mark,

In the case of *British Airways v Ryanair Ltd [2001]*, the claimant brought an action relating to 2 advertisements placed by Ryanair in 1999. The first ad carried the headline "Expensive BA--------DS!" The second ad sent out price comparisons between Ryanair and BA, showing Ryanair's prices as 1/5th cheaper than BA's.

The first "Bastard" ad had a limited run as the Advertising Standards Authority upheld a complaint from the public that it was "likely to cause serious widespread offence".

BA sued for trade mark infringement and malicious falsehood.

BA relied on various registered trade marks consisting of the letters 'BA'.

Justice.Jacobs said in his summing up that the primary objective of s10(6) of the TMA is to permit comparative advantage.

This case demonstrates that the courts are firmly of the view that the public are fully familiar with the concept of comparative advertising. This decision should provide some comfort to comparative advertisers who choose to employ ribald or hyperbolic language to ads, provided that they are careful to ensure that the substance of the advert is true.

Since 1994, UK courts have enthusiastically adopted the concept of comparative advertising. But since the EC Directive of 6.8.97, there are now 8 conditions which comparative advertising must comply with:

It must not be misleading.

It must compare like with like.

It must objectively compare one or more material, relevant, verifiable and representative factors of the goods or services in question.

It must not create confusion between the trade marks of the advertiser and those of the competitor.

It must not discredit or denigrate the trade marks or business of a competitor.

For products with designation of origin, it must relate in each case to products with the same "designation".

It must not take infair advantage of the trade mark or designation of origin of competing products.

It must not present goods or services as imitations or replicas of goods or services bearing a protected trade mark or trade name.

The definition given of comparative advertising within the directive is "any advertising which explicitly or by implication identifies a competitor or goods or services offered by a competitor".

Such ads, using more subtle means of identifying a competitor's product are not of course governed by s10(6) of the Act. Remedies would lie in actions of copyright infringement, passing off and trade libel.

Question 13

What are the principal objectives of Intellectual Property Law? Discuss commentators' views on the extent to which the law achieves its objectives?

Question 14.

One reason that Intellectual property law may fail to achieve its objectives is that these objectives are incompatible. Identify some potential areas of conflict and consider whether it can ever be possible to resolve such conflicts.

Question 15.

In relation to international intellectual property agreements, what kinds of interests come into conflict, and why?

Question 16.

Explain the significance of Intellectual Property Law for Indigenous peoples. Is this an appropriate vehicle for achieving their objectives?

Question 17.

Compare the roles of WIPO and WTO in the international management of intellectual property rights.

Question 18.

The first WTO decision on TRIPS in 1997 concerned India's approach to pharmaceutical patents. Explain the issues raised by the case and evaluate the WTO approach to these issues.

Question 19.

Examine the significance of the TRIPS agreement, particularly in relation to enforcement

Question 20.

What does counterfeiting mean, and what problems does it cause? Why is it necessary to achieve international agreement in tackling these problems?

Question 21.

IP-Copyright: exploitation and infringement; new technology.

A doll is made from a copyright drawing. Comment.

Answer:

Section 51 CDPA 1988 provides that it is NOT an infringement of any copyright in a design document or a model recording or embodying a design for anything other than an artistic work or a typeface to either make an article to the design, or to copy an article made to the design. The section removes copyright protection from the design of an article's shape or configuration, except where the article is (1) an artistic work in its own right, enjoying copyright under the Berne Convention; or (2) a typeface.

Under the transitional provisions, Schedule 1, paragraph 19 suspends for ten years after commencement the operation of section 51 in relation to designs recorded in a design document or embodied in an article prior to commencement. During the last of five of those ten years, licences will be available as of right to carry out the acts under section 51. Thus some copyright protection is preserved.

Section 52 says that where an artistic work has been exploited by or with permission of the copyright owner, by making an article through an industrial process, protection is limited to 25 years (section 52(1) and (2)) from the end of the calendar year in which the articles are first marketed.

Question 22.

How much of a work must be copied for an infringement action to take place?

Answer:

Copyright will not be infringed unless a substantial part is taken and used.

If an article is written using some copyright work, provided the writer of the article uses sufficient and independent skill and labour and has acknowledged sources, and does not use it for gain, then it is all right.

The court will look at the value of the material taken and the use made of it by the taker to decide whether the taker has created an original work of his own rather than an infringing copy.

In *Ladbroke v William Hill [1964] 1 WLR 273*, Lord Reid stated, "the question whether the defendant has copied a substantial part depends much more on the quality than the quantity of what he has taken."

Where an entire work has been appropriated, such as an unauthorised recording of a song or a piece of music, this is infringement, clearly.

Attempts to apply a percentage basis have been unreliable, indicating that the courts do not take a purely quantitative approach. In *Sillitoe v McGraw-Hill Books [1983] FSR 545*, appropriation of 5% of a novel amounted to a substantial appropriation.

In *Express Newspapers v Liverpool Daily Post and Echo[1985] WLR 1089*, Justice Whitford held that one-700th of a literary work copied by a defendant amounted to a substantial part of it.

In *University of London Press v London Tutorial Press [1916] 2 Ch 601*, Justice Peterson said "…what is worth copying is worth protecting."

So, it is not possible to identify a cut-off point. A single page may be sufficient, as in a football almanac, where copying one page explaining the off-side rule was an infringement, as in *Trengrouse v 'Sol' Syndicate[1901–4]MCC 13*.

In *Chappell v DC Thompson Magazines [1928–35] Mac CC 461*, four lines from a popular song used in an introduction to part of a serialised story were NOT a substantial infringement. There were some 80 lines in the original, but the court was clearly unimpressed by the content and considered that copyright should not be used as an instrument of oppression.

In the case of computer programs, *John Richardson Computers Ltd v Flanders and Chemtech Ltd [1993] FSR 497*, the court took the view that when considering substantiality, the similarities between the two programs, should be considered individually, and only then should the question whether the entirety copied was substantial be addressed. This was to be decided with regard to quality not quantity, taking into consideration originality and the distinction between idea and expression in asserting quality. In assessing substantiality, it was also necessary to filter out elements dictated by efficiency, external factors and elements in the public domain.

The avoidance of developing a fixed rule has been dictated by two factors. The first factor is that each case will turn on its facts and on legislation which applies to the wide varieties of work. The second factor is the existence of a wide range of permitted acts, and the fact that copying will not amount to an infringement if the use made of it constitutes a fair dealing for stated purposes, fair dealing itself a term not defined.

Assessed in terms of fair dealing, the quantity of material taken is but one factor in assessing whether there is actionable infringement, once the preliminary question of whether what has been taken is substantial. In *Hubbard v Vosper[1972] 2QB 84*, Lord Dillon suggested that it might be possible in some cases to take the whole of a copyright work and still fall within the concept of fair dealing. In such a situation however, the issue is the use to which the defendant has put the work after copying part of it, which is arguably of far greater importance than quality or quantity. Given that only a small amount needs to be taken to constitute infringement, arguably, use of the work is a better test.

Where fair dealing is used as a defence, whether too much has been taken is ultimately a matter of impression as in *PCR Ltd v Dow Jones Telerate Ltd (1999)*.

The whole work has to be looked at to determine whether the alleged infringing material has adopted the essential features and substance of the original.

Question 23.

Explain the 'fair use' defence in relation to research and private study.

Answer:

(a) Section 29(1) provides that fair dealing of a work for the purpose of research or private study does not infringe copyright in the work. The defence applies where the dealing takes place with literary, dramatic, musical and artistic works, as well as to the typographical formats of published works.

Special rules apply to the research or private study defence with respect to databases and computer prograMs. The rationale to this defence lies in the belief that research and study is necessary to generate new works. It also recognises that research and study does not normally interfere with the incentives and rewards that copyright provides to creators and owners.

In order for a defendant to rely on this defence they must show

- that the use made of the copyright work was for the purpose of research and study; and;

- that the dealing was fair. With the exception of databases, there is no need for the work and the author to be sufficiently acknowledged.

There is no requirement that the research or private study be for academic purposes. As such, it will potentially include situations where a person copies material to investigate their family history.

The research or private study need not be a non-profit activity. So the defence is available for commercial research.

ESSAY: TRADE MARK

Trade Mark

"In terms of the requirements for registration the 1994 Act represents a move away from the role of trademark law as a method of consumer protection and as a badge of quality".

Explain and critically evaluate this statement.

Introduction

"A trademark distinguishes the goods or services of one supplier from those of others. It is a badge of origin, a sign that indicates who made the goods or provided the services, and also serves to provide the consumer with a guarantee of quality."[172]

Trademark law still stresses that marks are indicators of origin, but whether it still protects consumers or can be seen as a badge of quality is debatable.

The changes made by the Trade Mark Act 1994 compared to the old Trade Mark Act 1938 will be analysed and case-law will be used to illustrate points.

The changes made by the Trade Mark Act 1994.

The Trade Mark Act 1994 made radical changes to UK trade mark law and improved the rights of the proprietor of a registered trade mark or his licensee. This is due to the requirements for registration under the 1994 Act. The Act brings UK trade mark law into line with that of the rest of the European Community, implementing Directive 89/104.

---

172 See the case of Aristoc Ltd v Rysta Ltd [1945] AC 68 in which the House of Lords emphasised the origin role of trademarks over their quality guarantee function.

Section 3 & 5 TMA 1994: presumption in favour of licensing.

The TMA 1994 contains a presumption in favour of registration and the Registrar no longer enjoys a wide discretion when considering whether to grant or refuse an application, subject to the grounds of refusal in sections 3 and 5 (see Appendix).

Section 1(1): what may be registered?

Unlike the TMA 1938, there are no positive requirements that a mark must fulfill other than being capable of graphic representation and of distinguishing goods and services of one undertaking from those of another.

This represents a great extension of what may be registered as a trade mark. Section 1(1) specifies that this can be any sign which is capable of being represented graphically and capable of distinguishing the goods and services of one undertaking from those of another.

For example, in *Ty Nant Spring Water Ltd.'s Trade Mark Application (2000)*, a sign, such as a sound or smell could be represented graphically even though interpretation or analysis might then be required to identify it. This was a case of application to register a "blue bottle" in Class 32 for "Bottled water, bottled mineral water, bottled spring water; bottles carbonated water". The mark was defined by reference to certain specified optical characteristics which sought to represent the particular cobalt blue colour of the bottle. The registrar did not allow it because the mark was not graphically represented and was devoid of distinctive character.

If an application is defective, there is no scope for amendment because of section 32(2) of the TMA 1994 and Rule 11 of the Trade Mark Rules 1994, now amended.

Every application has to dealt with on merit and not be reference to marks judged register-able on other occasions[173] When a trade mark application is refused by the registrar, a reapplication has to be taken in the Trade Marks Registry which has tightened up their procedure which now includes proper pleadings in line with the Civil Procedure Rules in the High Court and so cases must now be fully thought and set out at an early stage. It is now difficult to appeal from all first instance decisions—whether from High Court judges or from the Trade Marks Registry. The recent case of South Cone v Bessant and

---

173 See the case of AD 2000 Trade Marks (1977)

others shows how difficult it can be to overturn a hearing officer's decision.[174] This case illustrates how crucial it is to put all the evidence and arguments well in the first application for a trade mark.

The old system of Part A and Part B in the Trade Mark Register has been abolished and the TMA 1994 allows for registration of both signs of inherent distinctiveness, such as invented names, and marks which have achieved factual distinctiveness in the market.

Geographical names are now more easy to register. Under the TMA 1938, it was not possible to register a geographical name, no matter how distinctive, the most famous case being *In re York Trailer Holdings Ltd [1982]*[175]. It is now possible to register such marks, provided there is evidence of distinctiveness. However, it can be said that decisions have been made to allow geographical marks even when they are devoid of distinctiveness, as in the case of *Eurolamb Trade Mark [1997]*.[176]

Shapes can also now be registered, even packaging and 3-dimensional signs. In *Coco-Cola Trade Mark (1986)*, the House of Lords refused registration to the distinctive shape of the Coco-Cola product. But it would be successful today.

However, not every shape is registerable.

---

174 The case South Cone v Bessant and others involved the mark REEF. The applicants for the mark were a pop group called REEF who wanted to use the name for merchandising on clothes. The opponents owned the mark REEF for beachwear, particularly sandals. Mr. Justice Pumfrey upheld the opposition, overturning the hearing officer. He felt that REEF was a distinctive part of the opponent's mark and should be given more weight on the evidence than the hearing officer did. The case went to the Court of Appeal and Ca also decided that REEF was a distinctive part of the mark, but overturned the decision and upheld the Registrar's initial decision because it said that that initial decision was one that could be justified.

175 In re York Trailer Holdings Ltd (1982) 1 All ER 257, the Trade Mark Registrar appealed against a ruling allowing the registration of YORK, with a single maple leaf design without requiring the applicant to disclaim exclusive rights in the word YORK. The appeal was allowed.

176 EUROLAMB Trade Mark [1997] RPC 279.

Section 32(2)—defective application to registrar.

Exceptions listed under section 32(2) TMA 1994 include packaging which derives its shape from the goods fashioned, functional shapes and the shapes of packaging giving value to goods. There must be an addition to this requirement to achieve a technical result. Also, customers, not trade, must identify the goods as being from the undertaking. In the case of *Dualit*[177], registerability under section 1(1) and section 2(1) was fully argued before section 3(2) was even considered. and the application for the registration of a trade mark consisting of the shape of two toasters was refused since the shape was not distinctive. Justice Lloyd held that there was nothing about the shape alone which, apart from evidence of use, makes it inherently distinctive as a badge of origin of the applicant's products. The relevant class of persons is not trade buyers but the average customer of the product (pp 890,898. para.33). This clearly illustrates that the TMA 1994 still has consumer protection in mind.

Colours continue to be protected provided the mark is distinctive (*BP Amoco* case)[178]

Smells and sounds may be registerable although this has to be achieved by graphical representation. In the case of registration of odours, there is one significant case of *Venhootschap Onder Firma Senta Aromatic Marketing Application [1999]*[179], which, although not a UK case, has paved the way the successful applications in the UK.in *Sumitomo Rubber Co's Application Number 20014163*[180]. October 1994 and *Unicorn products' Application Number 200023431*[181]. In this case the applicant applied to register as an olfactory mark "the smell of fresh cut grass" for tennis balls. The application was initially rejected on the grounds that the words "smell of fresh cut grass" were not a graphical representation of the olfactory mark itself as required by Article 4 of the Community Trade Mark Registration.

Section 23: new rights; who can register a mark?

The TMA 1994 also introduced new rights to exploit a trade mark. Under section 23, any two or more persons, legal or human, can apply for joint registration of a mark. Before TMA 1994, joint registration of a mark was limited only to

---

177 Re Dualit Trade Mark [1999] The Times 19th July.
178 BP Amoco v John Kelly Ltd [2001]NI 25.
179 Venhootschap Onda Firma [1999] ETMR 429.
180 A registration of "a floral fragrance/smell reminescent of roses as applied to tyres".
181 A registration of "the strong smell of bitter beer applied to flights for darts".

partnerships because, under the 1938 Act, it was difficult to licence third parties to use registered trade marks without the trade mark owner risking losing rights in the mark because the licensee could have replaced the trade mark owner as the recognised commercial origin of the goods concerned. The 1994 Act has made it easier for the trade mark owner to license production or distribution under the mark without endangering the validity of the registration. But it is still important that the trade mark owner records licences and run checks to ensure the quality of goods or services provided by a licensee is high in order for the reputation of the trade mark to remain untarnished.

Section 24 licences

TMA 1938 s 28(6) prevented trafficking in the mark or character merchandising, where the mark was exploited for commercial gain other than to indicate a connection in the course of trade, but TMA 1994 frees a proprietor to license a trade mark for ALL the goods and services for which the mark is registered. TMA 1938 avoided use of the word "licence" and used instead "registered users". A licence is not effective unless it is written and signed by the grantor. TMA 1994 requires all register-able transactions such as assignments, licences and granting of security interests to be registered for security for the first time. This can only be in the interests of the consumer.

Section 50: certification for safety and quality of products.

Section 50 most of all, shows the incorrectness of Paul Torreman's statement.

Certification marks are registered under section 50 and Schedule 2 of TMA 1994. Certification marks were known under UK law before this, for example, the case of WOOLMARK and Colorcoat Trade Mark [1990][182] A certification mark for quality indicates that goods and services certified by the proprietor of the mark in respect of origin, material, mode of manufacture of goods or performance of services, quality, accuracy or other characteristics.

But the TMA 1994 extends the forms which a certification mark may take to include shapes, packaging, sensory marks and also services. Existing certification marks are preserved. Section 49 of the TMA 1994 also introduces the col-

---

182 Colorcoat Trade Mark [1990] B of Trade RPC 511.
　　It was held that the privilege of monopoly must not be given. The requirement of a trade mark is that it must be used to denote the source or origin of the goods in the course of trade.

lective mark, which differs from certification marks in distinguishing the goods and services of members of an association to which the proprietor of the mark belongs from those of other undertakings.

Such certification marks are register-able under a similar system to that of certification marks, with the exception that the absolute grounds of refusal under section 3(1) (geographical names) does not apply.

Section 103(2): new offence—oral misrepresentation.

The mark is protected from unauthorised use which is defined by section 103(2) as including use other than by means of graphics. So, for the first time, oral use of a mark is included, eg. catching the trader orally representing a mark as applying to goods and services. This complies with the Consumer Protection Act, Part 2.

Section 5(3): reputation

Most importantly, a significant change brought about by TMA 1994 is under section 5(3) where the Registrar may consider whether an application for registration will have a detrimental effect on the reputation or distinctive character of a well-known mark, even if the proposed registration is for dissimilar goods. The case, for example, of *Annabel's v Schock [1972]*[183] could not happen today because the defendant would not be allowed to register his business of escort agencies with the same name as the prestigious high-class night-club Annabel's in London.

TMA 1994 changes: from 'badge of quality to liberal stance to licensing'.

Under section 10(3), a registered proprietor is now able to prevent the unauthorised use of his trade mark in relation to goods or services which are not similar to the proprietor's goods or services, provided that the trade mark has a 'reputation' in the UK and that the unauthorised mark would take unfair advantage of or would be detrimental to the distinct character of the registered trade mark.

---

183 In Annabel's v Schock [1972] RPC 838(CA), the plaintiffs were the well-known night club in London. The defendant started an escort agency with the same name. The Court of Appeal granted an interlocutory injunction to stop the defendants using this name because the association of the high class night club with an escort agency would damage the night club's general goodwill to an unquantifiable extent.

The extension in section 10(3)(b) would prevent, eg. an imitation of a mark used for a soft drink being used as a weed-killer, and would protect brand names being extended or expanded into widely different products by deterring other traders from poaching existing goodwill. This is a sort of unfair competition step into the UK trade mark law.

TMA 1994 gives statutory basis for orders the courts may grant including erasure, removal or obliteration of the mark (s15(1)(a)) or destruction of the goods where it is not practical to erase the mark.

Section 41(1)© permits the registration of a series of trade marks which resemble each other as to their material particulars.

Whereas TMA 1938 was essentially concerned with the public interest mainly through protection from deceptive or misleading trade marks and strictly controlled licensing, refreshingly, TMA 1994 takes a more liberal stance to licensing. The responsibility now lies with the proprietor of a mark to ensure that the use of the mark by a licensee is not likely to deceive, risking revocation of his licence under section 46. The Registrar no longer does extensive examination; he limits his activities to recording details.

Section 92 makes it a criminal offence to apply a sign identical to, or likely to be mistaken for, a registered trade mark to goods or selling or hiring with such a sign.[184].

For the first time, there is a protection (s21 TMA 1994) against making threats other than for the application of a mark to goods or their packaging, the importation of goods and the supply of services. This is to prevent self-interest.

But it can be argued that section 10(6) TMA 1994 works against the interests of the consumer, as in the *Levi Strauss [2002]* case. On July 2002 the UK High Court gave summary judgement to Levi Strauss against Tesco Stores because Tesco infringed trade marks by importing Levi's jeans from outside the European Economic Area. (EEA). The case fell within section 10(6) TMA 1994 which permits use of a registered trade mark 'for the purpose of identifying goods or services as those of the proprietor or licensee (provided the use is not, for example, unfair or damaging). It is an interesting ruling as it breaches

---

184 Yet, before the TMA 1994, as in the case of R v Veys [1993] FSR 366, the application of a trade mark to goods does not necessarily amount to a trade description within the meaning of the Trade Descriptions Act 1968.

Tesco's right to own and dispose of property and the right to Freedom of Expression under the Convention for the Protection of Human Rights.

The court held that Tesco's property interests in the jeans was to be balanced against Levi's property interests in the trade mark. Similarly, Tesco's right to freedom of expression was subject to the protection of rights of others, which would include Levi's trade mark rights. The consumers were the ultimate losers because they were the beneficiaries of the lower prices at which Tesco was able to sell Levi jeans at due to buying from outside the EEA. This practice is called 'parallel importing' and the issue has been around since the 1938 TMA.

Another case in which the ECJ came down hard against the practice of 'parallel importing' is that of *Zino Davidoff v A & G Imports[1999]*. In this case, the defendant imported from Singapore genuine Davidoff perfumes for sale in the UK, presumably at a lower price than that of the legitimate distribution network. They had purchased a quantity of high-quality perfumes outside the EEA (Singapore), where wholesale prices were halved, and imported the goods into the EEA. The proceedings were for passing off and trade mark infringement. It is to be noted that before the EC Directive which instigated the TMA 1994, once goods were put on the world market they could generally be freely traded back into the UK, unless binding conditions specifying otherwise were inserted into all the goods' contracts for sale, or there was a difference between imported goods' condition and those generally sold in the UK.

It can therefore be argued that this ban on parallel importing which does not act in the interests of consumers who should be able to buy at the lowest prices, is merely a protection measure for trade within the EEA.

As regards consumer protection, it is not only price that matters ; health protection also matters and the UK government has recently been to the ECJ [185] to determine whether it could, since the EC Directive 2001/37, bring in a law to force tobacco companies to state the levels of tar, nicotine and carbon monoxide in their tobacco products instead of just the wording as at present of either "light", "low tar" or "mild" because these words could mislead the consumer into believing they were less harmful. The ECJ, on 13 the December 2002, said that the government could do so because some tobacco companies use such descriptors ("mild", "low-tar" or "light") as part of their trade marks.

---

185 R v Secretary of State for Health ex parte British American Tobacco, ECJ Case C-490/01[601J0491]

Section 42 TMA 1994 changes the registered period from seven years to ten years with renewable periods of ten years rather than the previous fourteen years in the 1938 Act, in keeping with the Madrid Protocol.

Conclusion

Today, a UK registered trade mark can provide a useful short cut to recognising a product which is worth buying from one which is not because a trade mark, since the TMA 1994, may be a word, logo, slogan, sound, smell or some physical feature of the goods for which the trade mark is used.

But since the introduction of the new law, some top brands are finding ways to protect themselves against look-a-likes by changing the colour scheme or the packaging.

There is also the issue of parallel imports as in the Levi jeans case where the brand owners insist that the retailers low-price tactics dilute the exclusive image of their goods and low-price retailers see it as breaking the selective distribution networks which keep prices at an inflated level.

The summary changes effected by the Trade Marks Act 1994 can be said to be that registration is now easier to obtain, the rights conferred by registration now extend to similar and dissimilar goods; the restrictive provisions for licensing have been removed and there is now only one register of marks.

This brings the conclusion that as far as consumer protection is concerned, it is still a matter of "caveat emptor" and as for the mark signifying quality, this is now a matter of extrapolating whether the mark on one high quality product means that that same mark on a similar or different product is also of high quality.

ESSAY: PERFORMERS' PROTECTION OF INTELLECTUAL PROPERTY

Critically evaluate the development of protection for performers

Introduction

From antiquity, possibly before even speech actually took place, humans used songs, often accompanied by rhythmic movements of the body or by some musical instruments, to convey a message that could otherwise not be expressed, or expressed poorly or ineffectively, with words.

This way of communication is effective because rhythm heightens the effect of words as it allows performers to convey them with a passion that words alone often cannot.[186]

Authorities, civil as well as religious, were quick to get control of these social moments when people forgot their daily troubles in those opportunities of social relaxation called festivals. The authorities have often lavishly remunerated those involved in the musical and scenic organisation because of the role that these moments have always played in preserving and fostering social cohesion and social grouping. But alongside these lucky protected performers, were those groups and individuals who were individual and creative and did not get remuneration but for the goodwill of the crowd they enthused. Today we would call the latter buskers and the former would have rights in performance.

In 1886, the Berne Convention for the Protection of Literary and Artistic Works was the first attempt at creating a set of rules with a validity extending beyond notional borders. [187] It gives a broad definition of "literary and artistic

---

186 http://leonardo.telecomitalialab.com/paper/WIPO99
   "Technologies for e-content"
187 Before this there was the English Copyright Act of 1709.

works" that applies to every production in the literary, scientific and artistic domain using a variety of expressions. (Article 2.1) [188]

The Berne Convention was revised in 1979 to address these key points of literary and artistic works:

a) The author has the right to claim authorship of the work and to object to any distortion or mutilation which would be prejudicial to his honour or reputation (Article 6 bis)

b) Different media are protected for different periods of time (Article 7).

c) Authors have the exclusive right to authorising the reproduction of their works, but reproduction of such works in certain cases are permitted. (Article 9)

d) Quotations from a work made available to the public are permitted. (Article 10-1).

e) Works can be used by way of illustration in publications, broadcasts or sound or visual recordings for teaching. (Article 10-2).

There are also universal conventions such as the Universal Copyright Convention of 1952, the International Convention for the Protection of Performing Artists, Producers of Phonograms and Broadcasting Organisations [THE ROME CONVENTION] of 1961, and the Convention for the Protection of Producers of Phonograms Against Unauthorised Duplication of their Phonograms of 1971.

---

188 Berne Convention Article 2(1) states:

"The expression "literary and artistic works" shall include every production in the literary, scientific and artistic domain, whatever may be the mode or form of its expression, such as books, pamphlets and other writings; lectures, addresses, sermons and other works of the same nature; dramatic or dramatico-musical works; choreographic works and entertainment in dumb show; musical compositions with or without words; cinematographic works to which are assimilated works expressed by a process analogous to cinematography; works of drawing, painting, architecture, sculpture, engraving and lithography; photographic works to which are assimilated works expressed by a process analogous to photography; works of applied art; illustrations, maps, plans, sketches and three-dimensional works relative to geography, topography, architecture or science."

The Copyright and Related Rights Regulations 1996

The Copyright and Related Rights Regulations 1996 introduced extensive new rights for performers by way of amendment to the Copyright, Designs and Patents Act 1988. Performers have performers non-property rights and recording rights. A performer's consent is required to exploit his or her performances. The Copyright, Designs and Patents Act 1988 defines "performance" as a dramatic or musical performance, a reading or recitation of a literary work, or a performance of a variety act or any similar presentation which is or so far as it is, a live performance given by one or more individuals. (section 180(1)).

Section 180(2) states that "a person having contractual recording rights in relation to a performance may take action in respect of any unauthorised recording of such performance"

But this Act was NOT retrospective.

Section 180 (3) says that any act done before 1/1/89 or in pursuance of arrangements made before that date is NOT to be regarded as infringing performers' rights or rights of persons having recording rights.

A performance qualifies for protection if it is given by a qualifying individual or if it takes place in a qualifying country (section 206).

A qualifying country includes the UK, other EC Member States and any country party to the ROME CONVENTION for the Protection of Phonograms[189].

Performers property rights and non-property rights.

Performers property rights subsist for a period of 50 years from the end of the calendar year in which the performance takes place (section 191(1)). An infringement of a performer's property rights is actionable by the rights owner

Performers also have non-property rights. These are the original rights under the Copyright, Designs and Patents Act 1988 to consent to the recording or line transmission of a performance and to importing, possessing or dealing

---

189 A qualifying country include those which the Rome Convention signed on October 26th 1961 and the Trade Related aspects of IP rights (TRIPS) agreement which was signed by 124 countries on the establishment of the WTO.

with the recording. Infringement is a breach of statutory duty and a right to seize illicit recordings[190] and sometimes criminal sanctions.

Non-property rights, like property rights, also subsist for 50 years maximum and performers' non-property rights are NOT retrospective before 1/1/96.

Permitted acts include fair dealing for the purpose of criticism, review or news reporting, incidental inclusion and things done for instructional, educational purposes or parliamentary and judicial proceedings. (section 189).

In Europe and the US.

Most European countries grant consumers the right to make private copies, based on the principle that these are NOT likely to compete with, and so reduce the market for, the original works. At the same time they accept a levy on recording equipment, including blank tapes.

In the US, there is the Audio Home Recording Act 1992 which grants consumers the ability to make private copies of broadcast music. The US copyright law has adopted the notion of fair use to include 4 parameters:

- character of use (eg. educational and non-profit purposes)

- nature of work (eg. factual as opposed to creative)

- portion of work (eg. small portion)

- effect on the market value of work (eg small impact)

WIPO Performances and Phonograms Treaty.

The UK's Copyright and Related Rights Regulations 1996 were due to the World Intellectual Property Organisation's conference on certain copyright and neighbouring questions, which also led to the adoption of two treaties, the

---

190 A recording for these purposes means a film or sound recording of the whole or substantial part of a qualifying performance. In the case of Bassey v Icon Entertainment plc [1995] EMLR 596, there is the issue of the wide definition of sound recording, capable of including "record", The making of a record from a master tape constitutes the making of a separate sound recording, requiring separate consent, but the court will look at the quality of the recording that has been taken rather than the quantity as in the case of LB Plastics v Swish Products Ltd.[1999] RPC 555.

WIPO Copyright Treaty and the WIPO Performances and Phonograms Treaty.[191] Both treaties extend some provisions of the Berne Treaty and add provisions which offer responses to the challenges brought about by information and communication technologies. So now,

- computer programs are protected as literary works;

- compilations of data and other material constitute intellectual creations;

- authors of computer programs; cinematographic and phonographic works have the exclusive right of authorising commercial rental of their works;

- authors have the exclusive right of authorising any communication to the public of their works by wire or wireless means;

- states that are party to the treaties provide legal remedies to those who alter Rights Management Information, ie, information which identifies the work of the author, the rights owners, information about the terms and conditions of use, and any numbers and codes that represent such information.

- states that are party to the treaties make it unlawful to have any device or component incorporated into a device or product in order to circumvent any process or mechanism or system that prevents or inhibits the exploitation of rights of rights holders.

Draconian penalties now in force.

In the UK, the new 2002 Copyright and Trade Marks Offences and Enforcement Act state that the court may make an order for forfeiture of illicit recordings and of destruction of unauthorised decoders with search warrants available to find same. It is a criminal liability to make or import an unauthorised decoder.

Although the UK might have brought in draconian penalties for IP infringements,. as regards computers world-wide, it is still difficult to stop illegal copying of copyright musical works by means of computer software.

In the recent case of BUMA/Stemra v KaZaA in Amsterdam, the court of appeal in Amsterdam reversed the decision of the District court which had

191 See Appendix 1.

ordered KaZaA to stop illegal copying of copyright musical works. KaZaA disseminates software which allows its users to find date files. download them and offer them to users. The exchange of MP3 files used for musical works is very popular. There are at least 17 million users of KaZaA software exchanging BILLIONS of files.

The Appellate Court held that it would be impossible for KaZaA to comply with the demand of BUMA/Stemra (the collecting society for copyright owners such as composers and lyricists) since, once it has allowed users to copy its software, KaZaA no longer has power to control its use and so dissemination of KaZaA siftware is NOT a tort and the infringement was committed by the USERS of KaZaA software and not be KaZaA itself.

Conclusion.

Although there is much legislation about, there is great difficulty in enforcing the legislation. Perhaps with the new enforcement Act, examples will be made in order to deter others.

BIBLIOGRAPHY

Books

Annand, Ruth & Norman, Helen, (1994), *Blackstone's Guide to the Trade Marks Act 1994*, Blackstone Press.

Bainbridge, David, (1998), *Cases & Materials in Intellectual Property*, 2nd. Ed., Pitman.

Bainbridge, David, (1999), *Intellectual Property*, 4th ed, Pitman.

Bentley L & Maniatis S, (1998), "Perspectives on Intellectual Property", Sweet and Maxwell Publishers.

Bentley L & Sherman B, (2001), "*Intellectual Property Law*", Oxford Press.

Bentley & Sherman, (2000), "*Intellectual Property*", Oxford University Press.

Bentley & Sherman, (2001), *Intellectual Property Law, Civil Procedure*, Volume 1 (2002), OUP, Sweet and Maxwell.

Cornish WR, (1999), "*Intellectual Property*"; 4th ed, Sweet & Maxwell.

Encyclopaedia of Forms & Precedents, (2002), "*Agreement between the proprietor of a newspaper or magazine and a contributor*", Butterworths.

Christie, A & S, Gare, (1998), *Blackstone's Statutes on Intellectual Property*, Blackstone Press, 4th. Ed., 1998

Christie A & Gare S, (2001), "*Statutes on Intellectual Property*", Blackstone.

Cornish, WR, 1999, *Materials on Intellectual Property* Sweet & Maxwell, 4th ed, Sweet & Maxwell.

Cornish, WR, 1999, *Intellectual Property Law,* Sweet & Maxwell, 4th ed, Sweet & Maxwell.

Holyoak, John & Torremans, Paul, (1998), *Intellectual Property Law*, 2nd. Ed., Butterworths.

Janis, Kay and Bradley, (1995), *European Human Rights Law*, Clarendon

Laddie, Prescott & Vitoria, (2000), *The Modern Law of Copyright and Designs*, 3rd Edition para 20.16.

Markensinis, B.S, (1990), *The German Law of Torts*, Clarendon Press. page 294-5.

Nelson, V, (2000), "*The law of entertaining and broadcasting*", Sweet and Maxwell.

Phillipson & Fenwick, (2000), *Breach of Confidence as a Privacy Remedy in the Human Rights Act Era*, 63 MLR 660.

Press Complaints Commission (UK), (1993), *Code of Practice*.

Reid, B, (1999), *A Practical Guide to Patent Law*, 3rd. Ed., Sweet & Maxwell.

Rickett, CEF & Austin, GW (2000) "International IP and the Common Law World", Harrt Publication.

Torremans, Paul & Holyoak, Jon (1996), *Butterworths Student Statutes—Intellectual Property Law*, Butterworths.

Wadlow C, (1995), "*The law of passing off*", Sweet and Maxwell Publishers

Internet Sources

http://www.wipo	for access to WIPO materials generally
http://www.wipo.int/clea	for intellectual property laws of 35 countries, the EC and WIPO
http://www.patent.gov.uk	UK Patent Office—for information on all aspects of intellectual property law
http://www.patent.gov.uk/design/legal/decisions	for patent office decisions re designs
http://www.patent.gov.uk/patent/legal/decisions	for patent office decisions re patents
http://www.patent.gov.uk/tm/legal/decisions	for patent office decisions re trade marks

http://europa.eu.int/comm/ internal_market/en/intprop/ index.htm	for European Community materials on intellectual property
http://europa.eu.int/eur-lex/en/	for European materials generally
http://wwwleonardo. telecomitaliab.com	Technologies foe e-content by Leonardo Chiariglione, CSELT, Italy.
http://216.239.35.120/translate	DVD's: The protections and the decoders, by A.B Pachelo.
http://wwwe.duncan-greham.com/ pages/internet.html	Copyright and Internet Law, by Duncan Greham, Solicitors.

Articles

Antill, Justine and Coles, Peter, (1996), *Copyright Duration: The European Community adopts 'Three Score Years and Ten',* 7 EIPR 379.

Blakeney, Michael, (1996), *The Impact of the TRIPS Agreement in the Asia Pacific Region,* 10 EIPR. 544.

Brimelow, Alison, (2001), *Does Intellectual Property Need a New Set of Wheels?* EIPR. Vol.23, Issue 1, January, p 44.

Chafee, (1945), "Reflections on the Law of Copyright I", 4 Columbia Law Review, 503 at p 507.

Christie, Andrew, (2001), *A Proposal for Simplifying United Kingdom Copyright Law* EIPR. Vol. 23, Issue 1, January 2001, p 26.

Cohen LJ, (1999), "*Is the English law of passing off discriminatory to Continental European Trade Mark Owners?*", EIPR.

Doherty, Michael and Griffiths, Ivor, (2000), *The Harmonisation of European Union Copyright Law for the Digital Age,* EIPR 17.

Endeshaw, Assafa, (2001), *Treating Intellectual Capital as Property: the Vexed Issues* EIPR. Vol.23, Issue 3, March, p. 140.

Firth A, (2001), "*Shapes as Trade Marks: Public policy, functional considerations and consumer perception*", EIPR.

Freshfields Bruckhaus Deringer, Solicitors, "*IP Update Autumn 2002*".

Gervais, Daniel J, (1999), *The TRIPS Agreement: Interpretation and Implementation*, EIPR. 156.

Golvan, Colin, (1999), *Aboriginal Art and Copyright: An Overview and Commentary concerning Recent Developments* [1999] EIPR 599.

Griffiths, Jonathan, (2000), *Lives and Works—Biography and the law of Copyright* Legal Studies, Vol. 20, No. 4, November, p 485.

Grosheide, F Willem, (2001), *Copyright Law from a User's Perspective: Access Rights for Users*, EIPR 321.

Harms, LTC, (2000), *Offering Cake for the South*, EIPR Vol.22, Issue 10 October, p 451.

Harvey, D Peter, (1993), *Efforts under GATT, WIPO and other Multi-National Organisations Against Trade Mark Counterfeiting*, EIPR, 446.

Kostecki, M (1991), *Sharing Intellectual Property Between the Rich and the Poor*, 8 EIPR 271.

Laddie, Mr. Justice, (1996), *Copyright: Over-strength, Over-regulated, Over-rated?* 5 EIPR 254.

Lewinski, Silke Von, (1998), *A Successful Step towards Copyright and Related Rights in the Information Age: The New EC Proposal for a Harmonisation Directive*, EIPR 135.

Linklater & Alliance, (2002), *"Intellectual Property News"*, Newsletter, May.

Macmillan, F & Blakeney. M, (1998), *The internet and communications carriers: copyright liability*, European Intellectual Property Review.

Macdonald-Brown, Charters and Ferera, Leon, (1998), *First WTO Decision on TRIPS* EIPR 69.

Mudiwa, Morris, (2002), *"Indigenous knowledge and IP rights: biodiversity resource rich, economically poor communities versus biodiversity resource poor, economically rich nations"*.

Phillips, Jeremy, (1999), *Fakin' It*, EIPR 275.

Riordan, Barrett J, (2000), *What's Driving Patent and Trade Mark Application Filings?* EIPR Vol.22, Issue 8, August, p 349.

Samuelson, Pamela (1999), *Challenges for the World Intellectual Property Organisation and the Trade-related Aspects of Intellectual Property Rights Council in Regulating Intellectual Property in the Information Age,* EIPR 578.

Stokes, Simon, (1996), *Copyright Legislation: Implementation of the EC Directive on term of protection of copyright* 3 EIPR D-80.

Vinje, Thomas C, (1999), *Copyright Imperilled?* EIPR 192.

Vinje, Thomas C, (2000), *Should we Begin Digging Copyright's Grave?* EIPR Vol 22, Issue 12, December, p.551.

Wiseman, Leanne, (2001), *The Protection of Indigenous Art and Culture in Australia: The Labels of Authenticity,* EIPR Vol.23 Issue 1, January.

APPENDIX 1

WIPO Performances and Phonograms Treaty 1996

(adopted by the Diplomatic Conference on 20th December 1996)

Article 1. Relation to Other Conventions.

(1) Nothing in this Treaty shall derogate from existing obligations that Contracting Parties have to each other under the International Convention for the Prorection of Performers, Producers of Phonograms and Broadcasting Organisations done in Rome, October 26,1961 (hereinafter the "Rome Convention").

(2) Protection granted under this Treaty shall leave intact and shall in no way affect the protection of copyright in literary and artistic works. Consequently, no provision of this Treaty may be interpreted as prejudicing such protection.

(3) This Treaty shall not have any connection with, nor shall it prejudice any rights and obligations under any other treaties.

Article 2. Definitions.

For the purposes of this Treaty:

a) "performers" are actors, singers, musicians, dancers, and other persons who act, sing, deliver, play in, interpret, or otherwise perform literary or artistic works or expressions of folklore;

b) "phonogram" means the fixation of the sounds of a performance or of other sounds, or of a representation of sounds other than in the form of a fixation incorporated in a cinematographic or other audio-visual work;

c) "fixation" means the embodiment of sounds, or of the representations thereof, from which they can be perceived, reproduced or communicated through a device;

d) "producer of a phonogram" means the person, or the legal entity, who or which takes the initiative and has the responsibility for the first fixation of the sounds of a performance or other sounds, or the representation of sounds;

e) "publication" of a fixed performance or a phonogram means the offering of copies of the fixed performance or the phonogram to the public, with the consent of the right-holder, and provided that copies are offered to the public in reasonable quantity.

f) "broadcasting" means the transmission by wireless means for public reception of sounds or of images and sounds or of the representation thereof,; such transmission by satellite is also "broadcasting"; transmission of encrypted signals is "broadcasting" where the means for decrypting are provided to the public by the broadcasting organisation or with its consent;

g) "communication to the public" of a performance or a phonogram means the transmission to the public by any medium, otherwise than by broadcasting, of sounds of a performance or the sounds or representations of sounds fixed in a phonogram. For the purposes of Article 15, "communication to the public" includes making the sounds or representations of sounds fixed in a phonogram audible to the public.

Article 3. Beneficiaries of Protection under this Treaty.

1) Contracting parties shall accord the protection provided under this Treaty to the performers and producers of phonograms who are nationals of other Contracting Parties.

2) The nationals of other Contracting Parties shall be understood to be those performers or producers of phonograms who would meet the criteria for eligibility for protection provided under the Rome Convention, were all the Contracting Parties to this Treaty Contracting States of that Convention. In respect of these criteria of eligibility, Contracting Parties shall apply the relevant definitions in Article 2 of this Treaty.

3) Any Contracting Party availing itself of the possibilities provided in Article 5(3) of the Rome Conventions or, for the purposes of Article 5 of the same Convention. Article thereof 17 shall make a notification as foreseen in those provisions to the Director General of the World Intellectual Property Organisation (WIPO).

Article 4. National Treatment

1) each Contracting Party shall accord to nationals of other Contracting Parties, as defined in Article 3(2), the treatment it accords to its own nationals with regard to the exclusive rights specifically granted in this Treaty and to the right to equitable remuneration provided for in Article 15 of this Treaty.

2) The obligation provided for in paragraph (1) does not apply to the extent that another Contracting Party makes use of the reservations permitted by Article 15(3) of this Treaty.

RIGHTS OF PERFORMERS

Article 5. Moral Rights of Performers.

1) Independently of a performer's economic rights, and even after the transfer of those rights, the performer shall, as regards his live aural performances or performances fixed in phonograms have the right to claim to be identified as the performer of his performances, except where omission is dictated by the manner of the use of the performance, and to object to any distortion, mutilation or other modification of his performances that would be prejudicial to his reputation.

2) The rights granted to a performer in accordance with paragraph (1) shall, after his death, be maintained, at least until the expiry of the economic rights, and shall be exercisable by the persons or institutions authorised by the legislation of the Contracting Party where protection is claimed. However, those Contracting Parties whose legislation, at the moment of their ratification of or accession to this Treaty, does not provide for the protection after the death of the performer of all rights set out in the preceding paragraph may provide that some of these rights will, after his death, cease to be maintained.

3) The means of redress for safeguarding the rights granted under this Article shall be governed by the legislation of the Contracting Party where protection is claimed.

Article 6. Economic Rights of Performers in their Unfixed Performances.

Performers shall enjoy the exclusive right of authorising, as regards their performances:

(i) the broadcasting and communication to the public of their unfixed performances except where the performance is already a broadcast performance; and

(ii) the fixation of their unfixed performances.

Article 7. Right of Reproduction.

Performers shall enjoy the exclusive right of authorising the direct or indirect reproduction of their performances fixed in phonograms, in any manner or form.

Article 8. Right of Distribution.

1) Performers shall enjoy the exclusive right of authorising the making available to the public of the original and copies of their performances fixed in phonograms through sale or other transfer of ownership.

2) Nothing in this Treaty shall affect the freedom of Contracting Parties to determine the conditions, if any, under which the exhaustion of the right in paragraph (1) applies after the first sale or other transfer of ownership of the original or a copy of the fixed performance with the authorisation of the performer.

Article 9. Right of Rental.

1) Performers shall enjoy the exclusive right of authorising the commercial rental to the public of the original and copies of their performances fixed in phonograms as determined in the national law of Contracting Parties, even after distribution of them by, or pursuant to, authorisation by the performer.

2) Notwithstanding the provisions of paragraph (1), a Contracting Party that, on April 15 1994, had or continues to have in force a system of equitable remuneration of performers for the rental of copies of their performances fixed in phonograms, may maintain that system provided that the commercial rental of phonograms is not giving rise to the material impairment of the exclusive rights of reproduction of performers.

Article 10. Right of Making Available of Fixed Performances.

Performers shall enjoy the exclusive right of authorising the making available to the public of their performances fixed in phonograms, by wire or wireless means, in such a way that members of the public may access them from a place and at a time individually chosen by them.

RIGHTS OF PRODUCERS OF PHONOGRAMS

Article 11. Right of Reproduction.

Producers of phonograms shall enjoy the exclusive right of authorising the direct or indirect reproduction of their phonograms, in any manner or form.

Article 12. Right of Distribution.

(1) Producers of phonograms shall enjoy the exclusive right of authorising the making available to the public of the original and copies of their phonograms through sale or other transfer of ownership.

(2) Nothing in this Treaty shall affect the freedom of Contracting Parties to determine the conditions, if any, under which the exhaustion of the right in paragraph (1) applies after the first sale or transfer of ownership of the original or a copy of the phonogram with the authorisation of the producer of phonograms.

Article 13. Right of Rental.

1) Producers of phonograms shall enjoy the exclusive right of authorising the commercial rental to the public of the original and copies of their phonograms, even after distribution of them by or pursuant to authorisation by the producer.

2) Notwithstanding the provisions of paragraph (1), a Contracting Party that, on April 15 1994, had and continues to have in force a system of equitable remuneration of producers of phonograms for the rental of copies of their phonograms, may maintain that system provided that the commercial rental of phonograms is not giving rise to the material impairment of the exclusive rights of reproduction of producers of phonograms.

Article 14. Right of Making Available of Phonograms.

Producers of phonograms shall enjoy the exclusive right of authorising the making available to the public of their phonograms, by wire or wireless means, in such a way that members of the public may access them from a place and at a time individually chosen by them.

COMMON PROVISIONS

Article 15. Right to Remuneration for Broadcasting and Communication to the Public.

1) Performers and producers of phonograms shall enjoy the right to a single equitable remuneration for the direct or indirect use of phonograms published for commercial purposes for broadcasting or for any communication to the public.

2) Contracting Parties may establish in their national legislation that the single equitable remuneration shall be claimed from the user by the performer or by the producer of a phonogram or both. Contracting Parties may enact national legislation that, in the absence of an agreement between the performer and the producer of a phonogram, sets the terms according to which performers and producers of phonograms shall share the single equitable remuneration.

3) Any Contracting Party may in a notification deposited with the Director General of WIPO, declare that it will apply the provisions of paragraph (1) only in respect of certain users, or that it will limit their application in some other way, or that it will not apply these provisions at all.

4) For the purposes of this Article, phonograms made available to the public by wire or wireless means in such a way that members of the public may access them from a place and at a time individually chosen by them shall be considered as if they had been published for commercial purposes.

Article 16. Limitations and Exceptions.

1) Contracting Parties may, in their national legislation, provide for the same kinds of limitations or exceptions with regard to the protection of performers and producers of phonograms as they provide for, in their national legislation, in connection with the protection of copyright in literary and artistic works.

2) Contracting Parties shall confine any limitations of or exceptions to rights provided for in this Treaty to certain special cases which do not conflict with a normal exploitation of the performance or phonogram and do not reasonably prejudice the legitimate interests of the performer or of the producer of phonograms.

Article 17. Term of Protection.

1) The term of protection to be granted to performers under this Treaty shall last, at least, until the end of a period of fifty years computed from the end of the year in which the performance was fixed in a phonogram.

2) The term of protection to be granted to producers of phonograms under this Treaty shall last, at least, until the end of a period of fifty years computed from the end of the year in which the phonogram was published, or failing such publication within 50 years from fixation of the phonogram, 50 years from the end of the year in which the fixation was made.

Article 18. Obligations concerning Technological Measures.

Contracting Parties shall provide adequate legal protection and effective legal remedies against the circumvention of effective technological measures that are used by performers or producers of phonograms in connection with the exercise of their right under this Treaty and that restrict acts, in respect of their performances or phonograms, which are not authorised by the performers or the producers of phonograms concerned or permitted by law.

Article 19...Obligations concerning Rights Management Information.

1) Contracting Parties shall provide adequate and effective legal remedies against any person knowingly performing any of the following acts knowing or, with respect to civil remedies, having reasonable grounds to know that it will induce, enable, facilitate or conceal on infringement of any right covered by this Treaty:

    (i)   to remove or alter any electronic rights management information without authority;

    (ii) to distribute, import for distribution, broadcast, communicate or make available to the public, without authority, performances, copies of fixed performances or phonograms knowing that electronic rights management information has been removed or altered without authority.

2) As used in this Article, "rights management information" means information which identifies the performer, the performance of the performer, the producer of the phonogram, the owner of any right in the performance or phonogram, or information about the terms and conditions of use of the performance or phonogram, and any numbers or codes that represent such information, when any of those items of information is attached to a

copy of a fixed performance or a phonogram or appears in connection with the communication or making available of a fixed performance or a phonogram to the public.

Article 20. Formalities.

The enjoyment and exercise of the rights provided for in this Treaty shall not be subject to any formality.

Article 21. Reservations.

Subject to the provisions of Article 15(3), no reservations to this Treaty shall be permitted.

Article 22. Application in Time.

Contracting Parties shall apply the provisions of Article 18 of the Berne Convention, mutatis mutandis, to the rights of performers and producers of phonograms provided for in this Treaty for that Party.

Article 23. Provisions on Enforcement of Rights.

1) Contracting Parties undertake to adopt, in accordance with their legal systems, the measures necessary to ensure the application of this Treaty.

2) Contracting Parties shall ensure that enforcement procedures are available under their law so as to permit effective action against any act of infringements and remedies which constitute a deterrent to further infringements

APPENDIX 2

APPENDIX 2 to Trade Mark Essay

Relevant Sections of the Trade Mark Act 1994

section 1(1)

In this Act a "trade mark" means any sign capable of being represented graphically which is capable of distinguishing goods or services of one undertaking from those of other undertakings.

A trade mark may, in particular, consist of words (including personal names), designs, letters, numerals or the shape of goods or their packaging.

section 2(1)

A registered trade mark is a property obtained by the registration of the trade mark under this Act and the proprietor of a registered trade mark has the rights and remedies provided by this Act.

section 3(1)

The following shall not be registered—

(a) signs which do not satisfy the requirements of section 1(1),

(b) trade marks which are devoid of any distinctive character,

(c) trade marks which consist exclusively of signs or indiscations which may serve, in trade, to designate the kind, quality, intended purpose, value, geographical origin, the time of production of goods or of rendering of services, or other characteristics of goods or services,

(d) trade marks which consist exclusively of signs or indications which have become customary in the current language or in the bona fide and established practices of the trade:

Provided that, a trade mark shall not be confused registration by virtue of paragraph (b), (c) or (d) above if, before the date of application for registration, it has in fact acquired a distinctive character as a result of the use made of it.

section 3(2)

A sign shall not be registered as a trade mark if it consists exclusively of-

(a) the shape which results from the nature of the goods themselves,

(b) the shape of goods which is necessary to obtain a technical result,

(c) or the shape which gives substantial value to the goods.

section 5(3)

A trade mark which-

(a) is identical with or similar to an earlier trade mark, and

(b) is to be registered for goods or services which are not similar to those for which the earlier trade mark is protected,

shall not be registered if, or to the extent that, the earlier trade mark has a reputation in the United Kingdom (or, in the case of a Community trade mark, in the European Community) and the use of the later mark without due cause would take unfair advantage of, or be detrimental to, the distinctive character or repute of the earlier trade mark.

section 10(3)(b)

A person infringes a registered trade mark if he uses in the course of trade a sign which-

(a) is identical with or similar to the trade mark, and

(b) is used in relation to goods or services which are not similar to those for which the trade mark is registered,

where the trade mark has a reputation in the United Kingdom and the use of the sign, being without due cause, takes unfair advantage of, or is detrimental to, the distinctive character or the repute of the trade mark.

section 10(6)

Nothing in the preceding provisions of this section shall be construed as preventing the use of a registered trade mark by any person for the purpose of identifying goods or services as those of the proprietor or a licensee.

But any such use otherwise than in accordance with honest practices in industrial or commercial matters shall be treated as infringing the registered trade mark if the use without due cause takes unfair advantage of, or is detrimental to, the distinctive character or repute of the trade mark.

section 15(1)(a)

Where a person is found to have infringed a registered trade mark, the court may make an order requiring him-

(a) to cause the offending sign to be erased, removed or obliterated from any infringing goods, material or articles in his possession, custody or control,

section 21(1)

Where a person threatens another with proceedings for infringement of a registered trade mark other than-

(a) the application of the mark to goods or their packaging

(b) the importation of goods to which, or to the packaging of which, the mark has been applied, or

(c) the supply of services under the mark,

any person aggrieved may bring proceedings for relief under this section.

section 32(2)

The application shall contain-

(a) a request for registration of a trade mark,

(b) the name and address of the applicant,

(c) a statement of the goods or services in relation to which it is sought to register the trade mark, and

(d) a representation of the trade mark.

section 41(1)(c)

Provision may be made by rules as to-

(c) the registration of a series of trade marks.

section 42

(1) A trade mark shall be registered for a period of ten years from the date of registration.

(2) Registration may be renewed in accordance with section 43 for further periods of ten years.

section 49

(1) A collective mark is a mark distinguishing the goods or services of members of the association which is the proprietor of the mark from those of other undertakings.

(2) The provisions of this Act apply to collective marks subject to the provisions of Schedule 1.

section 103(2)

References to this Act to use of a trade mark, or of a sign identical with, similar to, or likely to be mistaken for a trade mark, include use otherwise than by means of a graphic representation.

0-595-32927-6

www.ingramcontent.com/pod-product-compliance
Lightning Source LLC
Chambersburg PA
CBHW030937180526
45163CB00002B/600